Qualitative Educati In Action

Qualitative research is a key form of research in education; the findings of such projects frequently play a central role in shaping policy and practice. First time qualitative researchers require clear and practical guidance from the outset. However, given the diversity of both subject matter and methodological approaches encompassed by qualitative research, such guidance is not always easily come by.

Qualitative Educational Research in Action: Doing and Reflecting is a collection of ten first-hand accounts by education researchers of qualitative inquiries they carried out. The subjects are diverse, taking in school restructuring, policy analysis, critical literacy, phenomenology and the student–teacher relationship. Each chapter outlines the research question investigated and provides an overview of the project's findings, before going on to describe how each researcher approached the challenges of their particular inquiry. The researchers reflect upon the unexpected turns qualitative research can take and the way such projects can move through different theoretical and methodological positions, often ending up significantly removed from the original premise, but all the more valuable for that.

Anyone conducting qualitative research in education will be heartened and inspired by this collection, and will find in it invaluable guidance on dealing effectively with the idiosyncrasies and pitfalls of qualitative research – guidance that is all the more valuable for coming from those who have themselves navigated similar difficulties.

Tom O'Donoghue and **Keith Punch** are professors at the Graduate School of Education, University of Western Australia.

Qualitative Educational Research In Action

Doing and reflecting

Edited by
Tom O'Donoghue and
Keith Punch

Routledge
Taylor & Francis Group

LONDON AND NEW YORK

First published 2003 by Routledge
2 Park Square, Milton Park, Abingdon, Oxon, OX14 4RN

Simultaneously published in the USA and Canada
By Routledge
270 Madison Ave, New York NY 10016

Routledge is an imprint of the Taylor & Francis Group

Transferred to Digital Printing 2007

© 2003 Thomas A. O'Donoghue and Keith F. Punch

Typeset in Palatino by Wearset Ltd, Boldon, Tyne and Wear

British Library Cataloguing in Publication Data
A catalogue record for this book is available from the British Library

Library of Congress Cataloging in Publication Data
A catalog record for this book has been requested

ISBN 0–415–30420–2 (HB)
ISBN 0–415–30421–0 (PB)

Printed and bound by CPI Antony Rowe, Eastbourne

Contents

Contributors

Thomas A. O'Donoghue
Dr O'Donoghue is Professor in the Graduate School of Education, The University of Western Australia, where he is coordinator of the EdD programme. His research interests are in curriculum history and curriculum studies. He is the current President of the Australian and New Zealand History of Education Society.

Keith F. Punch
Dr Punch is Professor in the Graduate School of Education, The University of Western Australia, where he is Director of the School's International Programmes. His teaching fields are research methods (quantitative and qualitative), sociology of education and educational administration. His current research interests lie in education and social context, organisational behaviour and the internationalisation of education.

Elizabeth Tuettemann
Dr Tuettemann is a freelance researcher, writer, facilitator, educator and editor. She has authored and edited publications in several areas, including education, sociology, psychology, local history, medical science, scientific research and personal relationships. Her chapter in this book is based on her work for her award-winning PhD thesis written in the Graduate School of Education, The University of Western Australia.

Beverley Ward
Beverley Ward earned her Masters of Educational Management with Honours at the University of Western Australia. Her

chapter is based on the research she undertook there within the Graduate School of Education. She is currently furthering her Masters work on female professors as a scholarship PhD student. Her thesis, which is nearing completion, is entitled 'The female professor: a rare Australian species – the who and how'. The study provides generic and demographic data on female professors currently working in Australian public universities and their experiences and perceptions of reaching the apex of the academic hierarchy.

Lisa Catherine Ehrich
Dr Ehrich is a Senior Lecturer in the School of Learning and Professional Studies at Queensland University of Technology. Her main research interests lie in the field of educational leadership and management and the professional development of teachers and principals. She teaches in both the Master of Education and Bachelor of Education programmes and currently supervises a number of doctoral students.

Lesley Vidovich
Dr Vidovich is a Senior Lecturer within the Graduate School of Education, The University of Western Australia, where she is currently coordinator of the MEd Management degree. She teaches a range of university courses, from first year undergraduate to doctoral level, in the broad fields of educational policy and administration, sociology and politics of education, comparative education, and research methods. Her current research interests are in globalisation and education policy internationally at the higher education and schools' level.

Peter Stewart
Mr Stewart is a first class honours BEd graduate of the Graduate School of Education, The University of Western Australia. He is currently teaching in the English Department of Perth College, Mount Lawley, Perth. His chapter in this book is based on his research for his honours thesis.

Marnie O'Neill
Dr O'Neill is Dean of the Faculty of Education and Head of the Graduate School of Education, The University of Western Australia. She teaches in the fields of English education, language

literacy and learning, and teaching and learning studies. Her current research interests are in the areas of curriculum policy and practice, English education studies, and studies of gifted and talented children.

Helen Wildy

Dr Wildy is Associate Professor of Educational Leadership, Murdoch University, Perth, Western Australia. In the past decade she has taught and researched at the tertiary level in the areas of educational leadership and management, and school reform. Her research interests include school reform, restructuring, curriculum change, school leadership, performance management and, most recently, performance standards and assessments for school principals.

Tania Aspland

Dr Aspland is a Senior Lecturer in the School of Learning and Professional Studies at Queensland University of Technology. Her main research interests are curriculum leadership, thesis supervision and action research. She is currently assistant to the dean within her faculty.

Anne Chapman

Dr Chapman is Senior Lecturer in the Graduate School of Education, The University of Western Australia. Her teaching fields are pedagogy, mathematics education, and qualitative research methods. Her research interests are social semiotics and education, language and learning in school mathematics, and masculinities and mathematics.

Anthony Potts

Dr Potts is a Senior Lecturer in the Faculty of Education at La Trobe University, Bendigo, Australia, where he teaches social foundations of education and qualitative research methods courses. He heads the Education Studies area and coordinates the Master of Education (Research) and PhD programmes at his campus. His most recent project is published in his book *Civic Leaders and the University*, published by Peter Lang in 2002.

Chapter 1

The case for students' accounts of qualitative educational research in action

Thomas A. O'Donoghue and Keith F. Punch

The field of Education Studies has seen a burgeoning of post-graduate research student numbers in recent years. Many of these students are conceptualising their work within a qualitative research framework. In this, they are partly assisted by a wide range of methodological literature, including some excellent textbooks. Such works, however, while useful, do not help bridge the gap between principles of procedure and the final research plan. In particular, they do not give a sense of how postgraduate students mediate such principles and apply them to their unique research concerns. The situation is compounded by the reality that present-day qualitative research is characterised by diversity both in methodological orientation and in substantive topics of investigation. This is not to argue that students do not have ready access to a range of substantive research topics through reading reports on the research of others in unpublished theses and in academic journals. What are lacking, however, are works that bridge the divide between the methodological and the substantive, which give students ideas on how their particular research topic and their selected qualitative research approach can be brought together in a research project.

This book contributes to addressing the deficit in nine chapters covering a variety of topics and a variety of approaches to qualitative research. They describe the research approach adopted by postgraduate research students engaged in qualitative research projects. Each of the chapters opens with an outline of the research question investigated and a brief overview of the findings as reported in the writer's thesis. In each case they then go on, in different ways and in accessible language, to give an exposition on the sense made of the theoretical position(s) supporting the qualitative research approach chosen, on the manner in which they connected this position to their research topic, and on issues that arose in relation to their research design.

The chapters fall into three fairly loose groups. The first group, Chapters 2, 3 and 4, consists of accounts by researchers who remained relatively faithful to the central principles and methodological conventions of the qualitative approach that they used for their project. The second group, Chapters 5 and 6, is of accounts by researchers who also based their research projects on the central principles and methodological conventions of a qualitative research approach yet decided to 'push the boundaries' a little for various reasons, which they identify and justify. The third group, Chapters 7, 8, 9 and 10, consists of accounts by researchers who decided to 'push the boundaries' in a major way. Two of the researchers in question did so by oscillating between what some would consider to be mutually exclusive research positions, a third moved through three such positions as her study progressed, while the fourth decided to take the non-conventional approach within the humanities and social sciences to gaining a PhD by writing a book for publication rather than producing a standard thesis.

Chapter 2 is the first of the accounts by a researcher who remained faithful to the central principles and methodological conventions of the qualitative research approach within which she chose to locate her project. In this chapter, Elizabeth Tuettemann reports her experience of using grounded theory as the research approach chosen for her doctoral study on couple relationships and education. Two aspects of the study set it apart: the first is the choice of focus, the second the choice of research approach. The study is one of interpersonal relationships, and was motivated by evidence that students and teachers who experience disruption to, or disintegration of, the focal couple relationship at home are likely to function below capacity in the educational setting. The study was also set apart by the choice of grounded theory as the investigative approach for this area of research.

Chapter 3, by Beverley Ward, is also an account by a researcher who remained faithful to the central principles and methodological conventions of her chosen research approach – namely, the edited topical life history research approach. She provides background on the life history perspective, clarifies the meaning of life history, offers an understanding of the theoretical perspective of symbolic interactionism and its relationship with life history methodology, outlines the forms of life history, considers the assumptions and approaches underlying the life history research approach, details the data required to carry out the research, and presents possible guidelines to follow.

In Chapter 4, Lisa Ehrich untangles the threads and coils of what she terms the 'web of phenomenology'. As she discovered while undertaking her PhD study, to date there is considerable disagreement about what constitutes phenomenology and how it is practised. Her chapter has three main intentions: first, to clarify phenomenology as a philosophical movement by examining three of its major versions (i.e. transcendental, hermeneutic and existential phenomenology); second, to demonstrate the application of phenomenology as a research approach (writers from two dominant schools of thought which 'do' phenomenological research are compared and contrasted); and finally, to argue for the continuation of the tradition of phenomenological writing within education.

Chapters 5 and 6 are accounts by researchers who also based their research projects on the central principles and methodological conventions of a significant research approach, yet decided to 'push the boundaries' a little. In Chapter 5, Lesley Vidovich tells us that her PhD study focussed on the notion of 'quality' as a mechanism for increasing accountability to external stakeholders, which rose to prominence in the 1980s and 1990s as part of the New Right reform agenda of many national governments. She examined how the localised Australian context created a uniquely Australian version of a quality policy for universities. Using documents and interviews, the study analysed how the original ministerial policy of 1991 was recontextualised through the Higher Education Council, to the Committee for Quality Assurance in Higher Education (CQAHE), to individual universities over the 1990s. A theoretical framework of a policy trajectory consisting of contexts of 'influence', 'policy text production' and 'practice' (effects) at four different levels (macro, intermediate, micro and mini-micro) was employed. While this essentially follows a framework provided by Stephen Ball, a number of modifications were made to it in order to take into account both criticisms of his approach and the nature of the particular policy under investigation.

In Chapter 6, Peter Stewart and Marnie O'Neill outline some methodological considerations regarding a research project that aimed to identify and investigate the meanings that a group of Australian high school teachers of English attributed to critical literacy as theory and as a teaching practice. The project was undertaken in the interest of establishing some of the implications of these meanings for teachers and critical literacy theorists. The theoretical perspective of symbolic interactionism enabled the individual agency and responsibility of the participants to be taken into account. Working within such a framework, an adaptation of discourse analysis was used to analyse the data. This necessitated pushing the boundaries somewhat in an attempt to combine both perspectives.

Chapters 7, 8, 9 and 10 are accounts by researchers who decided to 'push the boundaries' in a major way. Helen Wildy's PhD study dealt with the dilemmas experienced by principals in dealing with the contradictions and pressures of school restructuring. In Chapter 7, she tells us that the portion of her thesis she most enjoyed writing was the methods section. She chose not to present this section as if she had conducted a neat, logical and linear study, as is usually done. Instead, she recounts a story of her dissatisfaction with the quantitative research approach, her flirtation with grounded theory and her decision to use the narrative account to present her data. Such a research story seemed more appropriate to the story she wanted to tell about school principals' struggle to deal with the dilemmas of restructuring. Moreover, she tried to give an honest account of her methodological journey, which would do more justice to the openness of principals whose stories she presented in the substantive part of her thesis.

Chapter 8, by Tania Aspland, arose out of her study that was designed to investigate the academic experiences of overseas students to understand better and illuminate the diverse nature of teaching, learning and supervision experienced by this relatively new student cohort enrolled in Australian universities. The specific purpose of the study was to report on and analyse the experiences of one such group, namely a diverse group of six women students from overseas countries enrolled in doctoral programmes in three Australian universities. It examined the supervisory experiences of the women as they completed their doctoral programmes over a three-year period, with particular reference to the social, cultural and political relations central to each supervisory partnership.

In confronting the inadequacies of existing research in the area, Aspland designed her study by making an 'epistemological break' with traditional research methodologies. She moved toward a pluralistic, advocacy-oriented, multiple-methods based research project. This methodological choice reflected her initial and ongoing commitment to thoroughness, with a desire to be open-ended and to take risks. The chapter describes the tensions and dilemmas she experienced as a methodological risk-taker as she moved through various phases of the study.

In Chapter 9, Anne Chapman describes how her research approach was developed at the 'point of need' in a study of how teachers and learners of school mathematics use language to construct mathematical meanings. A review of the literature identified a range of perspectives on the study of language and mathematics, classified under the headings of constructivism, social construction of meaning, mathematical discourse and the language arts movement. It was found that the different theoretical perspectives share a concern with four key factors in mathematics learning: cognitive, linguistic, social and contextual. The need, then, was to develop a theoretical framework that integrates these factors, a methodological position in line with that framework, and appropriate methods of data collection and analysis. The chapter details the work undertaken in this regard.

In Chapter 10, Anthony Potts offers a critical commentary on the research that resulted in the writing of his book *College Academics*, which was subsequently submitted successfully in fulfilment of the requirements for the award of the PhD by publication. The book is an insider study of the occupational socialisation of academic staff at one of Australia's oldest Colleges of Advanced Education.

The chapter belongs to the critical and reflective research genre that is at the core of qualitative social science research. It is a retrospective analysis of important issues that writing *College Academics* entailed, not all of which could be fully dealt with in the book itself. The chapter was prompted and shaped by international reviews of the book that have appeared in the literature. It is also a response to the call for writers and scholars to talk about their work, rather than from their work – to talk about the encounter between the self and the source materials, and the intellectual passions that sustained them.

Overall, these chapters will be of direct appeal to fellow students since they relate to work undertaken by their peers rather than by established academics. The first three chapters represent examples of the relatively standard application of accepted qualitative research approaches. Nonetheless, their value lies in their demonstration of the application of these approaches to particular research projects. In particular, they show how three postgraduate research students made meaning of them for their research questions, and how they ultimately organised their ideas logically.

The authors of the second group of chapters, while also having to make meaning of their chosen research approach, had the additional struggle of coming to terms with one or more other approaches. The challenge for them was to reconcile these other approaches with their original one, and to do so in a manner that was consistent and coherent. What we have are accounts of what ultimately made sense to them.

It is the third group of chapters that really demonstrates what is possible in qualitative research approaches in terms of their flexibility and their organic nature. They illustrate that often what really happens is that method and substance get developed together – that it is a mutually informing exercise. At least two of the chapters in this group also have the quality of giving a sense of the flavour of the intellectual journey. It is this area that presents the greatest challenge for the future. We would like to see additional studies further exploring this intellectual journey, thus complementing an existing corpus of such work by seasoned academic researchers.

Chapter 2

Grounded theory illuminates interpersonal relationships

An educator's perspective

Elizabeth Tuettemann

Introduction

The relevance of the quality and stability of interpersonal relationships in their home environment to those who teach and those who are taught can scarcely be overestimated. While the deleterious influence of unstable family relationships on the capacity of students to take advantage of educational opportunities is hardly in dispute, few if any studies have considered (except obliquely) the effects on their educational endeavours of teachers' and administrators' personal experience of fragmented family relationships. Knowledge of this deficit in the literature provided the stimulus for my PhD study. The choice of study theme arose from the premise that, for *all* participants interacting in the educational environment, the quality of the focal couple relationship in the home setting is highly relevant to the educational outcomes. For this reason a study that increased understanding of the processes involved in the sustaining or the disintegration of couple relationships was seen to be highly relevant to educational settings, and to the long-term educational outcomes. The research described here (Tuettemann, 1998) was thus motivated by a desire to contribute to the development of theory in the area of couple relationships, specifically to illuminate some of the processes involved in the building up and breaking down of relationships. It also offers constructs that fit the observable behaviours and outcomes in a much wider range of interpersonal interactions – including those in educational settings.

The substantive theory of 'fostering robustness in couple relationships' that I developed offers a fresh perspective on the attaining and sustaining of satisfying and lasting relationships, and provides a new set of theoretical constructs and a corresponding espousing–enabling model grounded in the data. The model, with its framework for understanding both the processes that occur for individuals and the outcomes for their relationships provides insights for those involved in marriage and *de facto* relationships, and is also relevant for those who provide education, counselling and therapy in this field.

In a departure from the more commonly used quantitative studies, which test theories, I sought to construct a theory from an exploration of how individuals in heterosexual couple relationships actually experience and manage these relationships. Using the constant comparative methods of grounded theory, I examined data from individuals who were (or had been) in couple relationships at various stages of development, maintenance, disintegration and rebuilding.

Central to the data collection were longitudinal studies (up to 5 years) using in-depth semi-structured interviews of 14 individuals, singly and together representing seven married couples and one divorcee. Supplementary primary data variously came from structured, semi-structured and informal interviews, observations and interactions in briefer engagements with some 170 rural and urban Australians. Further data and perspectives for comparison and refinement of the theory came from the literature and from consultation with key informants.

The initial focus was on a basic problem for individuals in heterosexual couple relationships – which I identified as that of the potentially damaging effects on their relationship of manifestations of emotional vulnerability. These fear-based attitudes and behaviours were mediated by a quest for a 'sense of personal sanctuary' – namely, personal immunity from the feared consequences of loss of face, or loss of approval by those whose acceptance was seen as important. Seeking to avoid the emotional pain of being exposed as foolish, inadequate or unacceptable, individuals were exhibiting a broad range of 'self-protective' and 'other-controlling' behaviours, including defensiveness and withdrawal, manipulation, withholding and attack (verbal, emotional or physical abuse). These behaviours had the potential to damage the relationship through diminishing resonance, depleting goodwill, eroding bonding and corroding commitment to the relationship ties.

Examining the patterns of response among individuals addressing this problem, I identified a core process, which I called *fostering robustness*. This process comprises a set of dual and intersecting sub-processes of personal orientation and personal development, namely 'espousing' and 'enabling'. The *espousing–enabling* model describes cognitions, strategies and behaviours typical of four levels of espousing, and four enabling/disabling transition phases that intersect with the espousing process. The four levels of espousing are: seeking sanctuary (espousing self); serving time (espousing the *status quo*, namely, perpetuation of the relationship); addressing dual needs (espousing a mutually sustainable relationship); and offering partner sanctuary (espousing partner empowerment). Providing transitions between the levels of espousing are the four phases of enabling: loss of hope/confidence; abandoning helplessness; consolidating confidence; and integrating strengths. According to the postulated espousing–enabling model, individuals in heterosexual couple relationships will, at any given time, be exhibiting one of these orientations or transiting (in either direction) through one of these phases. Together these processes address the opportunities for either growth or disintegration inherent in challenges to the individual's well-being in the relationship.

Why choose grounded theory?

Initially, I fully expected to use quantitative methods backed up by some preliminary qualitative explorations. To this end, after a year-long preliminary literature review, I spent some months trying to formulate the project by identifying and selecting variables and postulating relationships between them. In addition, I devised questionnaires and identified existing measuring instruments that addressed quality and stability of couple relationships, including those of Spanier (1976) and Snyder (1979). However, I eventually realised that this approach was not going to achieve the desired outcome, namely to gain understandings of factors perceived by couples themselves to be influential in their marital adjustment, and their well-being and satisfaction in their relationships.

I had no prior experience of grounded theory, but, in examining various research approaches, I became aware that it is noted for its rigour and provides a systematic way of constructing theories that illuminate human behaviour (Glaser and Strauss, 1967; Glaser, 1978; Glaser, 1992). It seemed that this research method was particularly suited to the extremely complex sets of human behaviour involved in heterosexual couple relationships.

Moreover, the use of this approach was also consistent with my intention, as a researcher, to elicit data that would, as far as possible, not be dependent on my own hypotheses or preconceptions. That is, I was not going to put before the participants a set of questions predicated on my hunches about what *might* be the issues for them. Nor was I placing boundaries and limits on their responses to my general questions, as happens when respondents are asked to choose between specific response categories. Herein lies the strength of the grounded theory approach; that the categories developed match the realities of those interviewed in that at each stage, as part of the analysis, the participants are involved in testing and verification both of the data and of the evolving theory. The extremely detailed and rigorous process of analysis, with constant recourse to comparison and checking, which is used to refine the constructs ensures 'the match between scientific categories and participant reality' (LeCompte and Goetz, 1982, p. 43).

Thus, in choosing grounded theory as the approach for this research into couple relationships, I had reason to expect that the theoretical 'model' I developed would reflect the realities of heterosexual couple relationships in the context of contemporary Australian circumstances. To this end, I set about gaining knowledge of and skills in this approach, beginning with broad reading of the academic literature on grounded theory, including research studies and reports using grounded theory and similar methods. My immersion in this discipline over more than four years continued with involvement in lectures, courses and seminars, and in establishing regular contact with other researchers for collaborative feedback and reciprocal analysis of data. This was augmented by membership of an on-line link-up with a qualitative research network.

I found it essential at all phases of the study to keep returning to the seminal writings of Glaser and others. During the period 1992 to 1998, several new works addressing grounded theory methodology were published and these provided additional insights. Among these were the writings of Daly (1992), Gilgun

(1992), Gilgun *et al.* (1992), Hutchinson and Wilson (1992, 1994), Kvale (1994), Melia (1996), Morse (1994), and Reissman (1994).

Having chosen grounded theory, I was ultimately faced with the dilemma of choosing between the Glaserian approach and that favoured by Strauss and Corbin (1990). In the event, the choice became almost automatic as the study progressed. Philosophically I had much more in common with Glaser's approach, with its emphasis on creatively exploring 'what is', rather than applying an elaborate algorithm as described by Strauss and Corbin. The latter left little room for conceptual creativity. Having come from a strongly scientific and quantitative background, I also found Glaser's rigorous approach and attention to elaborating a core category and exploring its variance more satisfying. Thus, in cases where they diverge, my study has been based on Glaserian rather than Straussian techniques.

Grounded theory in action – the essential elements

In grounded theory the whole process of data collection and analysis is a tightly-woven iterative process involving constant comparison, which leads to the gradual development and refinement of theory grounded in the data. This constant comparative method involves systematic 'cracking', coding and analysis of the data, beginning at the early stages of data collection. The outcomes of these analyses guide the subsequent data collection on the basis of the evolving hypotheses. This process of increasingly focussed data collection is called theoretical sampling.

The following essential elements of the constant comparative method became part of my research strategy: initial 'purposive' sampling; open coding of data; analysis by constant comparison; writing of memos; diagramming; theoretical sorting of memos; theoretical sampling; identifying a core category; integrating a central theoretical framework; selective theoretical sampling, coding and analysing; refining evolving theory; and reaching theoretical saturation. In the following paragraphs I elaborate on a few of these elements as they were exemplified in the study.

The source of the initial body of data was semi-structured interviews with individuals in heterosexual couple relationships, interviewed both singly and together, and selected on the basis of purposive sampling. I began by collecting data from young couples about to be married, and quickly expanded this to include data from individuals at various stages of marriage and in *de facto* relationships. This process of theoretical sampling led to the study of 'couple relationship' experiences of individuals in both rural and urban Australia and, ultimately, overseas.

In order to 'fracture' the data and identify as many categories as possible, I began open coding (analysis) of the data early in the research. As part of the data 'cracking' process, I repeatedly used Glaser's (1978, p. 57) basic set of questions governing open coding. They are, briefly:

1   What are these data a study of?
2   What category does this incident indicate?
3   What is actually happening in the data?
4   What accounts for the basic problem and process?

The analysis also involved constantly drawing comparisons between incidents and phenomena both within and between data sets, seeking to group them into categories and constructs of ever-increasing abstraction.

As the study progressed I followed Glaser's injunction: 'the *prime* rule is to *stop and memo* – no matter what [you] interrupt' (1978, p. 83). While generating scores of 'formal' memos, this strategy was also the mother of countless scribbled notes capturing inspirations that occurred when I was far from my desk, as well as numerous notes taped using my microcassette recorder while driving and while engaged in domestic tasks. The subsequent act of typing up these observational, theoretical, personal and methodological memos always generated a further bounty of insights. In like manner, the process of diagramming – devising schemas, 'maps' and flow charts demonstrating the relationships between categories, and links with other ways of describing the phenomena – was very significant to the development and depiction of the theoretical model. Theoretical sorting of these insights and memos was a crucial step to the theory building.

Theoretical sampling repeatedly involved the further collection and examination of data, guided by the emerging patterns. I was seeking data that contradicted, tested, corroborated or expanded the categories in order to refine the evolving theory. This also included regularly returning to the data already amassed, and interpreting and analysing it in new ways on the basis of the developing theory. As the study progressed, I recruited further individuals and couples as they were needed for theoretical sampling.

Once I had identified a theoretical code that offered a way of explaining how the substantive codes related to each other, I then focussed on integrating and 'fleshing out' the properties around a central core process. This selective coding strategy enabled me, over some months, to modify the theory in line with further input from a variety of sources and to improve its 'fit' with the observed and experienced reality of individuals in heterosexual relationships. As the theoretical framework developed and became more established, I increasingly used elements of the substantive literature as sources of secondary data. Further opportunities to test, refine and augment the developing theory came from key informants. Ultimately, data came from people with widely varying experiences of heterosexual couple relationships. When I reached the stage where additional data provided no new categories or properties of the categories, as they related to the core category or process, I considered that I had reached theoretical saturation.

A hierarchy of data sources

The data for the study came from a wide variety of sources, guided by the outcomes of the constant comparative method of analysis and the requirements of theoretical sampling. I categorised the data sources as primary, secondary or tertiary. The primary sources were individuals who supplied me with raw data through interviews, observations and interactions. The secondary sources of data came from the popular and professional literature, and included biographical and autobiographical accounts as well as published interviews and studies of people in relationship. I defined 'tertiary' data as those used for elaboration and refinement of the theory rather than for analysis (as in primary or secondary data directly related to couple interactions).

Primary data sources

Depending on the source of information, primary data collection was by means of structured or semi-structured in-depth interviews, informal impromptu interviews with couples and individuals, questionnaires, participant observation (Spradley, 1979, 1980; Wolcott, 1994), letters, facsimiles and telephone calls. The settings for primary data collection included homes, occupational and recreational settings, relationship and pre-marriage education groups, relationship enrichment groups, and rebuilding groups. While the main 'trunk' of primary data came from interactions with 14 individuals over periods up to five years, the total body of primary data ultimately included greater and lesser input from in excess of 180 rural and urban Australians born in Australia and overseas. They had experience of both satisfying and unsatisfying couple relationships, having variously experienced 'living together' and/or being engaged, married, separated, divorced, reconciled or remarried.

Secondary data sources

Supplementary data for analysis came from close examination of autobiographical literature and of other research studies into heterosexual couple relationships. There were also studies of individuals in relationships from the professional literature, and several published interviews with individuals about their relationships. In addition, data came from popular non-fiction, family chronicles, letters, journals, and media reports.

Tertiary sources

When the focus of the study shifted from analysis of 'raw' data to elaborating and refining the theory, tertiary sources of comparison and insight were provided by interactions and discussions with key informants such as marriage celebrants, academics, and professionals working in the areas of social work, relationship education and counselling. The study was also guided by increasingly focussed examination of both popular and scholarly literature as the theme of the study narrowed. Further tertiary data sources included statistical and research reports, media reports, and academic and popular literature.

Some practical and theoretical issues

From the outset, among the many factors influencing the design of the study was the reality that it is impossible to speak of a 'couple' operating in any particular manner, since even the most 'cohesive' of couples is ultimately two individuals. As Bernard (1982, pp. 4–5) comments:

> ... there is by now a very considerable body of well-authenticated research to show that there really are two marriages in every marital union, and that they don't always coincide.

Given that both partners in a couple relationship are likely to describe it differently, using non-congruent terms of reference, I chose to focus on 'individuals' in heterosexual couple relationships rather than upon 'couples' *per se*, and this guided my approach to data collection.

Choices in interviewing – as individuals or couples

Early in the study, I interviewed participants both with and without their partners. That is, for each couple selected the partners were initially interviewed separately within a short period of time, before being interviewed together. Subsequently, with those in the longitudinal studies I interviewed both partners together on most occasions, except when I was dealing with individuals who were no longer in a relationship, or who were unhappy in their relationship. This served a number of practical and methodological purposes, there being both advantages and disadvantages in conjoint interviews. Among the advantages were the convenience of having only one interview and the establishment and maintaining of trust – both knew exactly what the other was saying to me. Also, like Daly (1992, p. 8), I found that conjoint interviews tended to give a more reliable picture

> ... in that the bias in one version may be balanced by that in the other, spouses can jog one another's memory; and most important for reliability, spouses tend to keep each other honest.

I was also able to observe their verbal and non-verbal interactions and thus assess more readily what was happening between them than if only a one-sided perspective was being given. In any case, even when I was interviewing a couple together there were frequently opportunities for me to speak to them singly, since the normal household interruptions tended to take one or other partner away for several minutes at a time.

Daly (1992, p. 7) who interviewed couples rather than individual spouses (since his focus was on the 'couple' response to childlessness) expressed concern that couple interviews might not allow 'conflictual and embarrassing issues to emerge'. I found this fear largely unsubstantiated in my study, since by the time I had known a couple for a reasonable length of time they were raising conflictual and 'intimate' issues quite frequently.

Of more concern were the unanticipated disclosures. In a situation where one partner was clearly about to disclose something that might make the other uncomfortable, I would stop him or her and ask whether the non-disclosing partner wanted to continue, and/or to have the tape switched off. It was important to 'note and respect the boundaries' (Daly, 1992, p. 5). In addition, on occasions when a participant was showing some emotional arousal in response to the turn the conversation was taking, I would ask at intervals if he or she would rather stop there, or would like to stop the recording. Generally, the answer was no.

Practical aspects and techniques of data collection

The initial interviews with couples took place at my home. Subsequent interviews with those I identified as my primary participants (case-study individuals) took place either in their homes or in a location of their choice, which was sometimes a quiet room at their workplace or a secluded coffee shop. In the home setting there were occasionally interruptions in the form of telephone calls or visitors, but these were rare. My position was to use the opportunities these intervening events presented; real breakthroughs often came in these unlikely guises. The aim was to make the interviews as 'low key' and natural as possible. Further, I seldom 'forced' the conversation but let the individuals set their own pace and complete their train of thought. Particularly in the early stages of building my relationships with them, I was prepared to 'waste time' with 'digressions' since they often led to rich sources of data. The transcripts that eventuated were voluminous. However, as the study progressed I became more selective about the parts I examined in detail.

I commenced data collection using an *aide memoire* to guide the interviews unobtrusively while asking open-ended questions. The content of the interviews was focussed on the issues central to the research questions, but neither the wording nor the ordering of the questions was fixed. In order to avoid forcing the data, I simply encouraged the couples to tell me their 'relationship story' in their own ways, prompting them at times with questions focussed on their perceptions, responses and behaviours. The broad focus was on the evolution of their relationship to that point, its current status, specific highs, lows and turning points, and their hopes and expectations of themselves and their partners. With couples in relationships of longer standing, I explored their initial expectations of their relationship and their experiences of its evolution and current status. The data collection included personal observations of the individuals' verbal and non-verbal behaviour (including body language and voice intonations), along with their interactions with others, including their partners. This gave information about the status of their relationship.

For planned in-depth interviews I always used a microcassette tape recorder, and for other more impromptu interviews and conversations this was also my preferred option, as it freed me from note-taking and gave greater opportunity to be 'present' to the individual – and later repeatedly to listen to and reflect upon the conversation.

The researcher–participant relationship

I had no difficulty in recruiting participants for my study. They had a range of reasons, acknowledged and tacit, for taking part. Their acknowledged motivations varied from altruistic to self-serving, and a combination of both. Two young couples at various stages commented that they hoped and expected their involvement would be of use to others. One made it clear that they valued my presence as a potential support and 'counsellor'. Other individuals and couples enjoyed the opportunity to have a forum for their 'story' and for their views on marriages in general. My experience of participants' motivations paralleled that of Hutchinson and Wilson (1994, p. 306):

> Participants in research and therapeutic interviews do so for a variety of reasons such as achieving 'self-acknowledgement, self-awareness, catharsis, empowerment, as sense of purpose, social status, and looking good ... '

The first few couples came from my involvement with pre-marriage education, and as referrals from a marriage celebrant. Further participants came through self-selection when I appealed for volunteers while lecturing on marriage and relationship issues. Others volunteered when, at various phases of the study, I explained in general conversation what I was doing. Yet others were recruited by me for impromptu recordings when, in conversation, they would begin describing experiences or discussing issues that were of interest on the basis of my evolving theoretical framework. In the theoretical sampling phase not all of those who volunteered to take part were ultimately involved, as I eventually selected from the 'possibles' according to the theoretical sampling.

Establishing rapport

Establishment of rapport is advantageous in most qualitative studies, but is absolutely vital in a study of this kind where individuals and couples are invited to explore and reveal aspects of themselves and of their relationship that can be very personal and confidential. I chose to interview a relatively small number of couples in depth (alongside a multiplicity of briefer and more focussed informal interviews and conversations with other participants), fostering close interaction between myself and these participants. While this was time-consuming, the establishment of warm and trusting relationships with the individuals was most rewarding. In the words of Bernie Siegel (1988, p. 30), I became a 'privileged listener', and this is how I saw my role in the in-depth interviews with individuals and couples – or even with those who were talking in an impromptu manner about their relationships. It was also important to those speaking openly about their lives that they understood, trusted and respected my motives in doing the study. My readiness to disclose aspects of my own experience helped to generate trust.

Another essential part of the process of establishing trust and rapport was a patient, non-confrontational and low-key approach, which meant periods of unfocussed chat in the initial stages of each interview and also time given to 'long digressions' by participants during taping. This gave very lengthy transcripts.

It is hard to separate a consideration of the establishing of rapport from the issue of establishing credibility. In this case there were at least two aspects to the establishing of credibility; they were credibility as a professional person (a researcher) and credibility as an insider or 'one of us'. The former was never questioned, despite my deliberately low-key approach. Regarding the latter, my status as one who had been married twice and had survived marital vicissitudes was an advantage in establishing trust and rapport with my participants. Daly (1992) also found his insider status to be an advantage in his study of adoptive parents.

The researcher as insider/outsider

Much has been written about 'insider' and 'outsider' studies. This particular study was to some extent an 'insider' one, bearing in mind that my relationships with very young couples just beginning to explore their relationship were unavoidably different from my relationships with my age contemporaries in relationships of some duration or with experience of several relationships. Likewise, my relationships with individuals whose experience of couple relationships spanned longer periods than my own had slightly different overtones.

The accent was nevertheless on 'collaboration' with the participants as fellow explorers of the 'mysteries' of heterosexual couple relationships. This sense of joint exploration occurred as much with couples early in their marriage as it did with those married for some decades, and reflected my approach to the study participants; I was one of them, having experienced some of what they were experiencing, and learning alongside them. My self-disclosures to them reinforced this, as did my acknowledgement and thanks to them for advancing my own insights as they advanced their own. The question of 'insider versus outsider' raises issues of participant observation. There were elements of participant observation in my research, but this was not a dominant aspect of this study.

The researcher as instrument

In my interviewing I tried to maintain what Patton (1990, p. 58) calls empathetic neutrality:

> ... Empathy ... is a stance toward the people one encounters, while neutrality is a stance towards the findings. Neutrality can actually facilitate rapport and help build a relationship that supports empathy by disciplining the researcher to be non-judgmental and open. Empathy communicates interest in and caring about people, while neutrality means being non-judgmental about what people say and do during data collection.

As I listened to the interview tapes, I began reflecting on how my approach might come across to a participant. The first thing I noticed was that I tended to adapt my language to the language of those I was interviewing, particularly in terms of vocabulary and sentence construction. This, I decided, was not a bad thing, since it tended to minimise 'power and status' aspects and emphasise that I was, to some extent, an 'insider'.

Much later I also realised how similar my voice was to that of my sister. This caused me to reflect on the aphorism, 'it is not what you say but how it is perceived'. Aware of the tendency for her voice to put me on my guard, I began to listen to the tapes with a 'new' ear – that of a third person hearing the conversations. This time I was not only focussing on the input of the people I was interviewing, but was also studying my own input at a new level. I was becoming very aware of both what I said and how I used my voice as a researcher, as factors that might influence their responses.

Another potentially contentious aspect of 'researcher as instrument' is the question of subjectivity versus objectivity. Like Daly (1992) and Douglas (1995), I was conscious that my personal experience could predispose me to bias and preconceptions. On the other hand, one must ask whether someone who had no experience of couple relationships (a member of a celibate religious order, perhaps?) would have a better chance of producing unbiased findings. I suspect not. This general issue is addressed by several researchers, including Lightfoot (1983) and Heshusius (1994).

Multiple roles for the researcher?

Participant observer is only one of the roles that the researcher takes on, by choice or by default, willingly or reluctantly. I found, along with Daly (1992), how high the potential was for study participants to confuse the role of the researcher with the role of 'expert helper' or therapist. For me this was particularly the case with the young couples dealing with the early challenges of married life. Bearing in mind that it is reasonable and legitimate for the participants to expect some form of exchange for their service to the research, it became a matter of negotiating the positions from the outset and then considering each new situation on its merits. This meant that there were times when I became not just a researcher but also a 'resource' person – a professional with a certain level of experience and expertise, and with contacts and resources that could be accessed in times of crisis. In this, as in other cases, I was careful to delineate the limits of my expertise and to offer resources (such as booklists and referral). I also indicated that I was 'wearing the hat' of a concerned friend at the time. Several researchers have expressed opinions on this issue. Patton (1990, pp. 353–357) was adamant that:

> ... researchers using the in-depth interview have to tread the fine line between being unresponsive to the interviewees and their issues (and hence not establishing rapport) and being overresponsive (and hence catalysing more change than that which is absolutely inevitable as an outcome of the interview process). Above all it is necessary to be aware of this dimension of the data-collection process and to set clear limits.

The consensus was that, as Hutchinson and Wilson (1994) put it, researchers may occasionally step out of their researcher role to provide information or assistance to participants.

At times, one partner or the other would introduce a subject that they had not previously broached together and use our session together as an opportunity to air an issue. While both partners often reported that they found this beneficial, there were instances where this kind of behaviour elicited discomfort in the partner who was taken by surprise. One young couple in particular welcomed their sessions with me as an opportunity to talk over their relationship. Often one would turn to the other and say, 'I haven't told you about this, but ... '

Clearly, individual partners, to varying degrees, often saw the interviews as opportunities for airing of viewpoints in a safe atmosphere, resolving issues, raising other issues that might never be resolved, reporting changes in each other (generally positive ones), and having a difference of opinion with a witness adjudicator, impartial observer, adviser or referee. What role the researcher? And how often does that role change as the research progresses and according to the nature of the interaction with the participants?

These were just some of the questions that arose during the course of the study. Perhaps the most salient of the questions was whether I would choose grounded theory again for such a study.

Revisiting the choice of methodology: would I do it this way again?

The complexity of the area being studied was a major factor in choosing grounded theory for this study since it facilitated exploration of the many-faceted, kaleidoscopic interactions in couple relationships. Perhaps most importantly, it did not restrict the study participants in the data they offered since they were not asked to tailor their responses to a pre-packaged format. The choice of grounded theory had been in part driven by my own increasing frustration with aspects of quantitative research instruments. All too often, as both initiator and subject of research situations, I had felt trammelled by the boundaries imposed by these instruments, exasperated by the assumptions made and by the seeming irrelevance of much that was being explored through fixed questions and set response options.

Other researchers in this field have come to similar opinions. They include distinguished sociologist Norval Glenn, who expressed disappointment that for several decades researchers have tended to test simple propositions that don't advance our understanding of marriage. Although Glenn's research has been predominantly quantitative, he concluded (Glenn, 1990) that we need more qualitative research to generate new ideas. Glenn's perspective is strongly echoed by Helen Glezer (1997). Referring to her recent quantitative research, which had used telephone survey techniques, Glezer commented:

> Broad surveys don't give you the in-depth process stuff, which gives you a better feel of what is going on – what the issues are. [We] need to know about individuals ... we are working at a distance – we need more qualitative work.

In conclusion, in my opinion the choice of grounded theory was vindicated several times over. One of the most satisfying aspects was that it tapped into people's lives with a minimum of 'engineering' of circumstances and with a maximum of 'real' data collected in 'real' contexts. Hence the model that I constructed related closely to what individuals themselves perceived to be challenges to their well-being in couple relationships.

Bibliography

Adam-Smith, P. (1994) *Goodbye Girlie*. Ringwood, Victoria: Penguin Books Australia Ltd.

Bernard, J. (1982) *The Future of Marriage*. New York, NY: Yale University Press.

Conway, J. K. (1995) *True North: A Memoir*. London: Vintage.

D'Alpuget, B. (1982) *Robert J. Hawke: A Biography*. Middlesex, England: Penguin Books.

Daly, K. (1992) The fit between qualitative research and the characteristics of families. *In*: J. F. Gilgun, K. Daly and G. Handel (eds), *Qualitative Methods in Family Research*, pp. 3–11. Newbury Park, CA: Sage.

Douglas, J. D. (1995) *Creative Interviewing*. Beverly Hills, CA: Sage.

Gilgun, J. F. (1992) Definitions, methodologies, and methods in qualitative family research. *In*: J. F. Gilgun, K. Daly and G. Handel (eds), *Qualitative Methods in Family Research*, pp. 22–39. Newbury Park; CA: Sage.

Gilgun, J. F., Daly, K. and Handel, G. (eds) (1992). *Qualitative Methods in Family Research*. Newbury Park, CA: Sage.

Glaser, B. G. (1978) *Theoretical Sensitivity*. Mill Valley, CA: Sociology Press.

Glaser, B. G. (1992) *Basics of Grounded Theory Analysis: Emergence Versus Forcing*. Mill Valley, CA: Sociology Press.

Glaser, B. G. and Strauss, A. L. (1967) *The Discovery of Grounded Theory: Strategies for Qualitative Research*. New York, NY: Aldine Publishing.

Glenn, N. D. (1990) Quantitative research on marital quality. *Journal of Marriage and the Family* 52: 818–831.

Glezer, H. (1997) Work and family – work values, choices and participation. Cohabitation. Keynote address, National Marriage Education Conference, Brisbane, Australia, September 22–26.

Hasluck, A. (1981) *Portrait in a Mirror: An Autobiography*. Melbourne: Oxford University Press.

Hasluck, P. (1994) *Mucking About: An Autobiography*. Perth: University of Western Australia Press.

Hawke, H. (1992) *My Own Life: An Autobiography*. East Melbourne: The Text Publishing Company.

Hawke, R. (1994) *The Hawke Memoirs*. Port Melbourne: William Heinemann Australia.

Helfgott, G. and Tanskaya, A. (1996) *Love You to Bits and Pieces: Life with David Helfgott*. Ringwood, Victoria: Penguin Books Australia Ltd.

Heshusius, L. (1994) Freeing ourselves from objectivity: managing subjectivity or turning toward a participatory mode of consciousness? *Educational Researcher* 23(3): 15–22.

Hutchinson, S. and Wilson, H. (1992) Validity threats in scheduled semi-structured research interviews. *Nursing Research* 41(2): 117–119.

Hutchinson, S. and Wilson, H. (1994) Research and therapeutic interviews: a poststructuralist perspective. *In*: J. M. Morse (ed.), *Critical Issues in Qualitative Research Methods*, pp. 300–315. Thousand Oaks, CA: Sage.

Kvale, S. (1994) Ten standard objections to qualitative research interviews. *Journal of Phenomenological Psychology* 25(2): 147–173.

LeCompte, M. D. and Goetz, J. P. (1982) Problems of reliability and validity in ethnographic research. *Review of Educational Research* 52(1): 31–60.

Lightfoot, S. L. (1983) *The Good High School: Portraits of Character and Culture*. New York, NY: Basic Books.

Melia, K. M. (1996) Rediscovering Glaser. *Qualitative Health Research* 6(3): 368–378.

Morse, J. M. (ed.) (1994) *Critical Issues in Qualitative Research Methods*. Thousand Oaks, CA: Sage.

Neal, P. (1989) *As I Am: An Autobiography*. London: Arrow Books.

Park, R. (1994) *Fishing in the Styx*. Ringwood, Victoria: Penguin Books Australia Ltd.

Patton, M. Q. (1990) *Qualitative Evaluation and Research Methods*. Newbury Park, CA: Sage.

Reissman, C. K. (ed.) (1994) *Qualitative Studies in Social Work Research.* Thousand Oaks, CA: Sage.

Reynolds, D. (1988) *Debbie: My Life.* London: Sidgwick and Jackson.

Siegel, B. S. (1988) *Love, Medicine and Miracles.* London: Arrow Books.

Snyder, D. K. (1979) *Marital Satisfaction Inventory.* Los Angeles, CA: Western Psychological Services.

Spanier, G. B. (1976) Measuring dyadic adjustment: new scales for assessing the quality of marriage and similar dyads. *Journal of Marriage and the Family* 44: 731–738.

Spradley, J. P. (1979) *Participant Observation.* New York, NY: Holt, Reinhart and Winston.

Spradley, J. P. (1980) *The Ethnographic Interview.* New York, NY: Holt, Reinhart and Winston.

Stern, P. N. (1994) Eroding grounded theory. *In:* J. M. Morse (ed.), *Critical Issues in Qualitative Research Methods,* pp. 213–223. Thousand Oaks, CA: Sage.

Strauss, A. L. and Corbin, J. (1990) *Basics of Qualitative Research: Grounded Theory Procedures and Techniques.* Newbury Park, CA: Sage.

Tuettemann, E. (1998) Individual processes of espousing and enabling that foster robustness in couple relationships: a grounded theory study. Unpublished PhD thesis, The University of Western Australia.

Wolcott, H. F. (1994) *Transforming Qualitative Data: Description, Analysis, and Interpretation.* Thousand Oaks, CA: Sage.

Chapter 3

Reflecting on the value and use of the edited topical life history

A research approach

Beverley Ward

Introduction

My higher degree thesis, 'The Female Professor – A Rare Bird Indeed: Edited Topical Life History Portraits', provided an in-depth insight into a very small and elite group within the highest echelons of the Australian academic hierarchy – the female professor. This chapter offers some reflections on this often neglected type of research.

The aim of the study was to develop an understanding of the relationship between female professors' life histories, their ascent to their position within the higher echelons of the academic hierarchy, and the roles they play there. To this end, a central argument throughout the study was that certain events in our lives may be instrumental in shaping our attitudes and motivation with respect to our actions, present and future. An enhanced understanding of such phenomena is potentially germane to the study of the calling any person adopts, and his or her approach to that calling.

The study adopted the edited topical life history approach, which takes its theoretical impetus from that stream of qualitative research known as symbolic interactionism, which is both a theory and an approach to the study of human behaviour. Individuals cannot exist and develop in isolation from their environment, but different individuals in the same environment may react differently and their attitudes may change as circumstances change. It is the perceptions of the individual, rather than a definition of the facts by some external umpire, that will influence perspectives and actions.

The study drew on data obtained from intensive interviews

with three female professors on the academic staff of Australian public universities. Using a thematics approach, a number of themes emerged (recurrent patterns of related issues emanating from the data): backgrounds – family and schooling; significant others – the influence and support they received from role models, mentors, partners and friends; the notion of a career, and whether it was planned; their perception of a professor's role; leadership – their style, thoughts, convictions; the gender factor – their perception of the difference between male and female professors, the different expectations placed upon them and the way their performance is assessed; the struggle and the price – the hurdles and challenges they have faced; and the changing gender balance in the university population – their views on whether there should be more female professors and why, and why they think there are so few female professors. The professors also offered words of advice to female students and academics.

It is relevant here to note that the study was undertaken at a time when Australian higher education is facing unprecedented challenges. It is challenged by budget cuts and the increasing need to become self-funding, it is adjusting to meet the needs of an increasingly diverse student population, it is responding to the impact of global competition, and it is struggling to come to terms with the implications of new technology. Within the Australian context today a wide divergence in gender balance exists, both in terms of the academic staff as a whole and of the ratio between academic staff and the student population. Females represent over half of all undergraduate students enrolled in higher education. Paralleling the increase in female undergraduates has been a dramatic, albeit much slower, increase in the number of females engaged in graduate study (DEET, 1993). However, despite the adequacy of the current pool of potential female faculty, their entry into faculty ranks on a full-time basis (and in particular to the rank of full professor) continues to be disproportionately low. Simply put, the higher the level in the academic hierarchy, the lower the percentage of females represented there.

A life history perspective

In the 1930s and 1940s, under the influence of Ernest Burgess and Robert Park, sociologists trained at the University of

Chicago employed the life history method extensively (Becker, 1966). However, since this period little attention has been paid by mainstream researchers to the life history approach, the emphasis being placed instead on quantification and empirical measurement.

There seems to be no clear reason why the life history has been so neglected, especially when, as asserted by Watson and Watson-Franke (1985; pp. 203–204), individuals' effect on 'smaller, more homogeneous society [such as the family and community] ... may be of considerable importance'. The study of life histories is 'not just to understand the idiosyncrasies of individual experience'; rather, researchers 'may also find that life histories offer us precise documentation about how individuals, in the process of changing their lives for themselves, also alter the environment for others and thus act as significant agents of change'.

A revival of interest in the life history method in sociology started in the 1970s, at about the same time that symbolic inter-actionism was becoming popular again. This is borne out by the appearance and increasing number of qualitative research method books that include life history methods. Examples include Taylor and Bogdan's *Introduction to Qualitative Research Methods* (1984); Denzin's *The Research Act* (1970); Schwartz and Jacobs' *Qualitative Sociology* (1979); and Lancy's *Qualitative Research in Education: An Introduction to the Major Traditions* (1993). This resurgence of interest in the life history method (Faraday and Plummer, 1979; Goodson, 1980; Bertaux, 1981) can be attributed to its capacity to provide greater depth to the participants' perspectives than other forms of research.

Goodson (1980, pp. 66–67) further asserts that the life history's greatest strength lies in its penetration of the subjective reality of the individual, allowing the 'participant to speak for herself or himself'. A well-documented life history creates a backdrop against which we can amplify, and better understand, raw information. It helps us to add 'why' and 'how' dimensions to the 'what' of empirical data. This is important if we are to inter-pret the data from a personal perspective rather than simply carry out an operational and predictive analysis. The specific significance of the life history method is that it addresses the interactions that ultimately direct the participant's line of thought and subsequent courses of action, enabling the researcher to identify and comment upon the genesis of the directions being researched. In reviving the life history, it is important to see the sociological enterprise as multifaceted. Becker's image of the mosaic is useful – 'each piece added to a mosaic adds a little to our understanding' (Goodson, 1980, pp. 66–67).

The language of the method

Minichiello *et al.*, (1990, p. 146) define LIFE as the unfinished process of the lived experiences of a person, and as being given meaning by that person and his/her significant others; HISTORY is an account of an event or events, including an attempt to explain why it occurred; TOPICAL is, in this context, defined as a single instance, phase or subject; and EDITED is the process of interpreting and preparing a text for publication. The 'topic', in the 'edited topical life histories' developed in the study discussed in this chapter, was the interaction between the perceptions and factors that had influenced the female professors and their entry into the higher echelons of the academic hierarchy.

The life history is exactly what it says it is – the history of an individual's life given by the person living it and solicited by the researcher. It is a sociological autobiography obtained from solicited narratives and/or in-depth interviewing. It is an endeavour to acquire an account of a person's life told in his or her own words. The life history can be regarded as different from traditional autobiographies because it is acknowledged that in the autobiography the author provides only what he or she wishes the reader to know. In the life history, what is 'read is mediated by the researcher's interaction with the person during the telling of the story, the coding, analysis and interpretation of it' (Minichiello *et al.*, 1990, p. 147).

The life history presents the experiences and definitions held by one person, one group or one organisation as this person, group or organisation interprets those experiences. Becker describes it aptly when he writes that it is 'a faithful rendering of the participant's experience and interpretation of the world he lives in' (1966, pp. v–vi).

On this, the distinction between the life history and the life story is important to understand. It is essentially a question of context, and the key factor is the element of collaboration with an external observer. The life history reviews a wider range of evidence than the simplistic life story – the 'story we tell about our life' (Goodson, 1992, p. 6). The life history, by placing the life story in its historical context, enables the researcher to draw conclusions about the factors determining the participant's thoughts, actions and motivation.

What is an edited topical life history?

Forms of life history

Three basic forms of the life history can be distinguished: the complete, the topical, and the edited (Allport, 1942). All the forms, however, contain three central features: the person's own story of his or her life; the social and cultural situation to which the participant and others see the participant responding; and the sequence of past experiences and situations in the participant's life. Ultimately, differentiation depends on the aims of the research process, what the researcher is looking for and/or trying to illustrate, and the degree of intrusion made by the researcher in the creation of the final document.

Complete life history

The complete life history attempts to cover the entire life (from birth) experiences of the participant. It will more than likely be long, complex, and many-sided. Shaw's life history of a juvenile delinquent (1966), for example, was made up of some 200 pages and was followed by a sociological interpretation. A careful and studied representation of one person's, one organisation's or one group's entire life experiences is the central feature of the complete life history (Denzin, 1978, p. 217).

Topical life history

The topical life history shares all the features of the complete form except that only one phase or aspect of the participant's life is presented. Sutherland (1937), for example, in a presentation of the life of a professional thief, was concerned only with the experiences of one thief as these related to the social organisation of professional crime. The work simply provides one man's conception of his profession, with interpretations and annotations offered by Sutherland to clarify unusual terms and phrases; there was little reference to other sources or documents. However, this is not to imply that the topical life history never employs additional sources.

The topical life history can take either the comprehensive or limited mode. The comprehensive topical life history mode does not try to focus on the full life history, but rather examines a particular issue/subject. Good examples of complete topical life histories are Shaw's (1966) study of 'Stanley', examining his delinquency; Sutherland's (1937) depiction of the professional thief using Chic Conwell's information; Hughes' (1961) study of Janet Clark and her drug use; and Bogdan's (1974) research of Jane Fry's trans-sexuality. The limited topical life history is actually the same as a complete topical life history, except that less material is covered. Usually these life histories will include more than one person per volume.

Edited life history

The edited life history may be either topical or complete. Its key feature is the continual interspersing of explanations, comments and questions by someone other than the focal participant. Sutherland, for example, approached an edited life history by adding interspersed passages and annotations. Some degree of editing and interspersion of comments by the observer must be present for theory construction and hypothesis testing. Without this, 'the life history must stand as its own sociological document' (Denzin, 1978, p. 218). A relatively recent example of an edited topical life history is Dimmock and O'Donoghue's (1997) *Innovative School Principals and Restructuring: Life History Portraits of Successful Managers of Change.*

Editing topical life histories

At this point it is appropriate to discuss the process of 'editing' the topical life history. Editing is the form that interpretation takes in the written presentation of life histories, and occurs in the presentation of all forms of life history. Editing can range from minimal interpretation by the researcher (such as cutting out the verbal repetitions and the 'ums' and 'ahs') through to extensive cutting of the account and arrangement in chronological sequence, to 'verification by anecdote' (Plummer, 1983, p. 115) where the use of selected quotes from the informant's interviews are used as examples to illustrate and accentuate the theoretical position being argued by the researcher.

In many cases, editing is carried out with the purpose of easing the work of the reader. Allport's (1942) advice that while unique styles of expression, including argot and colloquial phrasing, should remain unedited, editing for the sake of clarity or to remove repetitious material would seem justified.

Assumptions

There are four assumptions inherent in the life history research method (Denzin, 1978, p. 216). These are:

1   The primary assumption is that human conduct is to be studied and understood from the perspective of the persons involved. All data that reflect upon this perspective should be employed. This is a case for actively sharing in the participant's experiences and perspectives and taking the role of the 'acting other'. If this role is not taken, the researcher could slip into the fallacy of objectivism by substituting the researcher's interpretations for the interpretations of those studied.
2   The sensitive observer employing this form of research method will be concerned with relating the perspective elicited to definitions and meanings that are lodged in social relationships and social groups. The variable nature of these definitions across situations will also be examined.
3   Concern will be directed to recording the history of one person's, one group's or one organisation's experiences. This feature becomes a hallmark of the life history – the capturing of events over time. Hence the researcher becomes a historian of social life, be it the life of many persons similarly situated or the life of one person.
4   Because this form of research method presents a person's experiences as he or she defines them, the objectivity of the person's interpretations provides fundamental data for the final report. The researcher must first determine the participant's 'own story'.

Approaches

The two basic approaches that underpin the life history method are the nomothetic and the idiographic (Allport, 1942). The nomothetic approach is based on the concept that theoretical generalisations are drawn from systematic experimentation, usually employing quantitative research methods in an attempt to establish general laws or principles: 'It assumes social reality is objective and external to the individual'(Burns, 1994, p. 2) and should be 'applicable to many individuals' (Minichiello *et al.*, 1990, p. 155). The ideographic approach 'emphasises the importance of subjective experience of individuals, with a focus on qualitative analysis' (Burns, 1994, p. 3). Social reality is regarded as a creation of individual consciousness, with meaning and the evaluation of events being a personal and subjective construction.

Minichiello *et al.*, (1990, p. 155), state that the two approaches can be seen as complementary, and 'in the course of acquiring and analysing the contents of a series of life histories, and searching for patterns within each one, the researcher may purposefully or serendipitously uncover patterns between them'. The type of life history in which the researcher engages will in turn be dictated by the approach adopted, which will be dictated by the reasons for and aims of focussing on a particular individual case. My study took an ideographic approach.

The data

Life history materials include any records or documents, including the case histories of social agencies, that throw light on the subjective actions of individuals or groups. These may range from letters to autobiographies, newspaper accounts to court records, and interview transcriptions to personal diaries. This material can be classified into two basic forms of data; public archival records and private archival records.

Public archival records, which are prepared for the express purpose of examination by others, include actuarial records, political and judicial reports, governmental documents, and media accounts (Denzin, 1978, p. 219). Private archival records, the most important data source for the life history, consist of autobiographies, questionnaires, interviews and verbatim reports, diaries, memoirs, logs and letters, as well as photographs, films, self-observations and possessions. The autobiography is the most common form of personal document, and there are three forms that correspond to the three types of life history: comprehensive, topical, and edited (Allport, 1942). Allport (1942, p. 77) asserts that 'the great merit of the autobiography is that it provides the "inside half" of the life; the half that is hidden from the objectively-minded scientist'. Hence it provides a photograph of the participant's life that is neither fully apparent nor fully public.

If a comprehensive life history is to be written, public archival records should be combined with private and personal data. Unfortunately, according to Denzin, few researchers using the life history method use a combination of data sources to adopt a triangulation strategy, preferring to use only interviews, or the analysis of letters or autobiographies. My study on female professors only utilised interviews, owing to time constraints.

The guidelines

Some guidelines must be established if life histories are to be used for the purpose of comparison, although there seems to be little consensus on the form these guidelines should take. Denzin (1978, p. 229) asserts that 'some set of uniform standards must be established, but that they should be broad enough to permit each investigator to adopt them to specific cases'.

There are several proposals on how to approach the life history method, such as Dollard's, whose formulation directs attention to early family influences on the participant while pointing to the impact of cultural settings in the developmental process; Denzin's, who proposes a more focussed format (and largely mirrors that of Young); and Young's (Denzin, 1978). Young's guideline is probably the most elaborate and lengthy, being divided into the following areas: data on the family (including the participant and his or her father and mother); developmental history of the individual, including experiences confronted in childhood, preadolescence, adolescence and adult life; and the nature and meaning of the inner (subjective) life, including such topics as emotional stabilities, sense of the self, power devices, recreational and avocational activities, basic satisfactions, and work as a value (Denzin, 1978, p. 230). The approach used in my study on female professors reflected that used by Lemert in 1951 in his study on the life history of deviants (Denzin, 1978). The strength of Lemert's proposal lies in its emphasis on the natural history of events over time and the consideration of religion, social class, and political and social climate.

Life history and symbolic interactionism

As stated earlier, my study on female professors took its theoretical impetus from that stream of qualitative research known as symbolic interactionism. Before elaborating on the relationship between symbolic interactionism and the life history method of research, it is worthwhile providing an outline of the theoretical position of symbolic interaction.

Theoretical framework of symbolic interactionism

My work on life histories, and in particular edited topical life histories, takes its theoretical impetus from qualitative research. This is based on the Chicago School of Symbolic Interactionism, developed by Herbert Blumer, which continues the classical Meadian tradition that 'sees the self as socially constructed ... It is not possible for a self to arise outside of social experience' (Potts, 1997, p. 7). The symbolic interactionist theory is influential in Australia, the United States and Great Britain (Potts, 1997).

At the heart of symbolic interactionism are three principles that govern, and in turn are governed by, beliefs about the nature of the self, of meaning and of symbols. The three principles are formulated by Blumer (1962, p. 2) as follows:

1   'Human beings act towards things on the basis of the meanings that the things have for them'. Blumer uses 'things' to cover a range of recipients of behaviour from the concrete (that is, people, material objects, and institutions) to the abstract, which includes the situations in which one finds oneself and the principles – in the sense of ideals – that guide human life

2   'The meaning of such things is derived from, or arises out of, the social interaction that one has with one's fellows'. This is seen as a 'continuous process' by Woods (1992, p. 338)

3   'Meanings are handled in, and modified through, an interpretive process used by the person in dealing with the things
he [*sic*] encounters'.

Hence, for the symbolic interactionist, the meaning of each thing,
abstract or concrete, is not fixed. Rather, it is constantly being
adjusted in line with new information. This information is of all
kinds, and the new meaning has its effect on human acts. So
meaning is acquired from our experience of the world, and,
because we are in constant engagement with the world, meaning
is constantly being modified, if not completely changed.
However, while 'our interpretive scheme may be shared by all
people, it may be associated with only one group or even be personal' (Woods, 1992, p. 338).

Meltzer *et al.* (1975, p. 1) summarise the position:

> Thus, 'symbolic interaction' is the interaction that takes place
> among the various minds and meanings that characterise
> human societies. It refers to the fact that social interaction
> rests upon a taking of oneself (self-objectification) and others
> (taking the role of the other) into account.

They stress that the most basic element in this image of human
beings is the notion that society and the individual are inseparable units; that while it may be possible to separate the units
analytically, the fundamental assumption is that a complete
comprehension of either one demands the comprehension of the
other. Meltzer *et al.* (1975, p. 2) emphasise the following:

> In the interactionist image ... [t]he behaviour of men and
> women is 'caused' not so much by forces within themselves
> (instincts, drives, needs, etc.) but by what lies in between, a
> reflective and socially derived interpretation of the internal
> and external stimuli that are present.

During the last 30 years, the symbolic interactionist perspective
and the qualitative research methods that came with symbolic
interationism have become very popular in academic sociology
(Davis, 1966; Wild, 1974; Connell, 1985).

The relationship

In sociology, the use of personal documents and life histories has been related to symbolic interactionist theory and to the perception that life histories are useful in providing 'the salient experiences of a person's life and that person's definitions of those experiences' (Taylor and Bogdan, 1984, p. 78). In fact, it has been argued (Schwartz and Jacobs, 1979; Plummer, 1983) that there is a fundamental affinity between the central tenets of symbolic interactionism and life history research.

There are three theoretical assumptions that are common to life history research and symbolic interactionism:

1   Life is viewed as a concrete experience – meaning there is no point in studying abstractions of individuals or of social life; the central consequence is that 'in every case of study, we must acknowledge that experiencing individuals can never be isolated from their functioning bodies and their constraining social world' (Plummer, 1983, p. 54). Cooley (1956, p. 152) illustrates the importance of recognising that 'a separate individual is an abstraction unknown to experience, and so likewise is society when regarded as something apart from individuals'.

2   Life is regarded as an ever-emerging relativistic perspective. This means that 'the reality shifts with a person's life and people act towards things on the basis of their understandings, irrespective of the "objective" nature of those things' (Plummer, 1983, p. 56).

3   Life is viewed as inherently marginal and ambiguous – 'if we have taken one person's subjective reality seriously in a life history, and then consider it in relation to another person's, then there is always the possibility that ambiguity and incongruity will become evident in their definitions of the same situations' (Minichiello et al., 1990, p. 153).

Minichiello et al. (1990, p. 164) point out that 'life histories constitute a significant strategy in incorporating history within the theoretical framework of symbolic interactionism'. This is achieved, Plummer (1983, p. 70) argues, by 'the changing biographical history of the person and the social history of his or her lifespan'. This is evident in what Minichiello et al. (1990,

p. 164) classify as the 'career' mode of life histories, 'which is derived from symbolic interactionism and focusses on the changing meaning of an individual's life course as he or she moves through personal crises side-by-side with a given age cohort in an evolving historical culture'.

Woods (1993, p. 450) clarifies the connection between the theoretical position of symbolic interaction and the life history research method when he stresses the living connection between the past and present, the life of which comes from the development of current meanings and interpretations over time:

> The present has a living connection with the past. Current meanings and interpretations are shown to have grown and developed over time. In tracing ... [individuals'] own histories, we acquire a fuller, deeper and richer understanding of them. Examining the interrelationships of incident, thought, people and place that underpin the current person provides a context that is just as relevant as, if not more than, the prevailing social, institutional and situational.

Conclusion

The life history, after a long period of neglect, is re-emerging strongly as a significant research tool. The local detail and the everyday life of any person will prove to be a rich and useful source of knowledge about that person. Those who hope to understand the action of specific groups must, at some stage, study the action of individuals within those groups.

Life history is unique as a method of social research, as it deals with human experiences such as feelings, action and talk as they happen within the confines of the social structure specific to the historical period in which the participant lives. Hence it is a means of focussing on the relationship between biography, structure and history (Minichiello *et al.*, 1990, p. 164). The constant criticism of life histories has been that they are too individualistic, neglect the broader historical context and, on this basis, are not theoretically useful. This criticism has been made without taking into account that the life history enables us to view the totality of the biographical experience.

The significance of the life history is that it enables an appreciation of how a person reacts, not in finite terms but in the context of his or her environment. This same person might have reacted differently faced by different social, political, psychological or religious influences. In practical terms, this means we have a tool to help us develop theories about the underlying factors that motivate the participants of our research when they are faced by certain sets of circumstances.

The usefulness and significance of the life history method is based on the notion that it provides 'an account of individual experience which reveals the individual's actions as a human agent and as a participant in social life' (Blumer, 1939, p. 29). Based on this central tenet, life histories constitute a significant strategy in incorporating history within the theoretical framework of 'symbolic interactionism'. The individual cannot exist and develop in isolation from his or her environment, but different individuals in the same environment may react differently, and their reaction may change as circumstances change.

It is the interpretations of the individual, rather than a definition of the facts by some external umpire, that will influence perceptions and actions. Perception is reality. Thus, different individuals will place different interpretations on an identical set of circumstances, and may be motivated to act in very different ways. The identification of individuals' interpretations, and the way in which these interpretations may affect their perceptions and actions, is the very essence of the life history as a research tool.

While many eminent proponents of the life history discipline have attempted to provide guidelines that will apply an element of uniformity to bodies of research gathered by this approach, there appears to be little consensus concerning the form these guidelines should take, other than that it must be sufficiently flexible to allow the researcher to adapt the information gathered to the case in point.

Social history attests to the predicable cyclic nature of successful social movements, yet those involved in them rarely look to the experience of others as part of their strategic efforts to effect change (Lie *et al.*, 1990). Every generation has to learn the lessons of the past or repeat the mistakes. A life history, in whatever form, can make a valuable contribution to the learning process by giving us 'both a glimpse of ourselves and a reflection of the human spirit [in that it] illuminates history, inspires by examples, and fires the imagination to life's possibilities' (Horner, 1987).

Bibliography

Allport, G. W. (1942) *The Use of Personal Documents in Psychological Research*. New York, NY: Social Science Research Council.

Becker, H. S. (1966) Introduction. *In*: C. Shaw (ed.), *The Jack Roller: A Delinquent Boys Own Story*. Chicago, IL: University of Chicago Press.

Bertaux, D. (ed.) (1981) *Biography and Society: The Life History Approach in the Social Sciences*. Beverley Hills, CA: Sage.

Blumer, H. (1939) *An Appraisal of Thomas and Znaniecki's The Polish Peasant in Europe and America. Critiques of Research in the Social Sciences*. New York, NY: Social Science Research Council.

Blumer, H. (1962) Society as symbolic interaction. *In*: A. M. Rose (ed.), *Human Behaviour and Social Processes*, pp. 1–5. Boston, MA: Houghton Mifflin.

Bogdan, R. (1974) *Being Different: The Autobiography of Jane Fry*. New York, NY: John Wiley.

Burns, R. B. (1994) *Introduction to Research Methods*. Melbourne: Longman Australia Pty Ltd.

Connell, R. W. (1985) *Teachers' Work*. Sydney: George Allen and Unwin.

Cooley, C. H. (1956) *Human Nature and the Social Order*. Glencoe, IL: The Free Press.

Davis, A. F. (1966) *Private Politics: A Study of Five Political Outlooks*. Carlton: Melbourne University Press.

DEET (1993) Female academics. Higher Education Series, Report No 18. Department of Education, Employment and Training.

Denzin, N. K. (1970) *Sociological Methods: A Sourcebook*. Chicago, IL: Aldine Publishing Company.

Denzin, N. K. (1978) *The Research Act: A Theoretical Introduction to Sociological Methods*. New York, NY: McGraw-Hill Book Company.

Dimmock, C. and O'Donoghue, T. A. (1997) *Innovative School Principals and Restructuring: Life History Portraits of Successful Managers of Change*. London: Routledge.

Faraday, A. and Plummer, K. (1979) Doing life histories. *Sociological Review* 27(4): 773–789.

Goodson, I. (1980) Life histories and the study of schooling. *Interchange* 12(4): 62–76.

Goodson, I. (1992) *Studying Teachers' Lives*. London: Routledge.

Horner, M. S. (1987) The Radcliffe Biography Series. *In*: R. Coles (ed.), *Simon Weil: A Modern Pilgrimage*, p. 27. Reading, MA: Addison-Wesley.

Hughes, H. M. (1961) *The Fantastic Lodge: The Autobiography of a Girl Drug Addict*. Boston, MA: Houghton-Mifflin.

Lancy, D. (1993) *Qualitative Research in Education: An introduction to the Major Traditions*. New York, NY: Longman Cheshire.

Langness, L. L. and Frank, G. (1981) *Lives: An Anthropological Approach to Biography*. Novato, CA: Chandler and Sharp Publishers, Inc.

Lassey W. R. and Sashkin, M. (eds) (1983) *Leadership and Social Change*. San Diego, CA: University Associates, Inc.

Lie, S. S. and O'Leary, V. E. (eds) (1990) *Storming the Tower: Women in the Academic World*. London: Kogan Page.

Meltzer, B. B., Petras, J. W. and Reynolds, L. T. (1975) *Symbolic Interactionism: Genesis, Varieties and Criticism*. London: Routledge.

Minichiello, V., Aroni, R., Timewell, E. and Alexander, L. (1990) *In-Depth Interviewing: Researching People*. Melbourne: Longman Cheshire.

Plummer, K. (1983) *Documents of Life: An Introduction to the Problems and Literature of a Humanistic Method*. Sydney: Allen and Unwin.

Potts, A. (1997) *College Academics*. Charlestown, New South Wales: William Michael Press.

Schwartz, H. and Jacobs, J. (1979) *Qualitative Sociology: A Method to the Madness*. London: Collier Macmillan.

Shaw, C. R. (1966) *The Jack Roller: A Deliquent Boy's Own Story*. Chicago, IL: University of Chicago Press.

Sutherland, E. H. (1937) *The Professional Thief by a Professional Thief*. Chicago, IL: Phoenix Books.

Taylor, S. J. and Bodgan, R. (1984) *Introduction to Qualitative Research Methods – The Search for Meaning*. New York, NY: John Wiley and Sons.

Tuchman, B. (1979) Biography as a prism of history. *In*: M. Pachter (ed.), *Telling Lives: The Biographer's Art*. Philadelphia, PA: University of Pennsylvania Press.

Watson, L. C. and Watson-Franke, M.-B. (1985) *Interpreting Life Histories: An Anthropological Inquiry*. New Brunswick, NJ: Rutgers University Press.

Wild, R. A. (1974) *Bradstow: A Study of Class Status and Power in a Small Australian Town*. Sydney: Angus & Robertson.

Woods, P. (1985) Conversations with teachers: some aspects of life history method. *British Educational Research Journal* 11(1): 13–26.

Woods, P. (1992) Symbolic interactionism: theory and method. *In*: M. D. LeCompte, W. L. Milroy and J. Preissle (eds), *A Handbook of Qualitative Research in Education*. London: Academic Press.

Woods, P. (1993) Managing marginality: teacher development through grounded life history. *British Educational Research Journal* 19(5): 447–465.

Chapter 4

Phenomenology

The quest for meaning

Lisa Catherine Ehrich

Introduction

That professional development is one of the most challenging and important activities facing school principals and their staff has been highlighted in the policy and professional development literature. The central purpose of my PhD was to explore the nature of professional development from the unique experiences of principals. It was felt there was a need to understand professional development outside the confines of theoretical constructs and overarching frameworks. A phenomenological methodology, therefore, guided the study and allowed the principals' experiences to speak for themselves. Following the work of Giorgi (1985a, 1985b), a phenomenological psychological approach was used to analyse the data. Three significant findings were raised for further comment, and these related to the mismatch between current policy directions for professional development and the reality of principals' experiences; the principals' conceptualisation of professional development as a planned and unplanned activity; and principals as curriculum leaders.

Throughout my research I became acutely aware that there is considerable disagreement about the meaning of phenomenology and that its definition has yet to be settled. For example, it has been defined as an 'overarching perspective' that includes qualitative research (Maykut and Morehouse, 1994, p. 3), yet Merriam and Simpson (1984, p. 89) argue the converse and view it as an orientation that falls within qualitative research. Furthermore, it has been defined as a substantive philosophy (following the works of philosophers such as Husserl, Merleau-Ponty and

Heidegger) and a distinctive approach to the study of a range of disciplines (Embree and Mohanty, 1997, p. 10). It seems that part of the disagreement about the meaning of phenomenology can be attributed to the fact that the term has been used so widely. As Patton (1990, p. 68) suggests, phenomenology has been referred to as a philosophy, a paradigm and a methodology, and has been equated with qualitative methods of research. Such wide usage can only create tangles of meaning.

This chapter is based on my intellectual struggles to construct a methodological framework to guide my PhD research. I attempt to illuminate the philosophical underpinnings of phenomenology and identify two key approaches that have used the phenomenological perspective in particular ways. The main intention of the chapter is to untangle some of the conceptual threads and coils that make up the web of phenomenology. This is done in order to present a more accessible way of understanding what has been described as 'one of the major philosophical movements of the twentieth century' (Embree and Mohanty, 1997, p. 1).

The chapter is divided into five main parts, with each part corresponding to the metaphor of phenomenology as a web. The first part provides an overview of the metaphor. The second part begins with an explanation of Merleau-Ponty's (1962) 'phenomenological method', which he sees as providing an entrance through which we can access phenomenology. Four of the key components that constitute phenomenology are described. The phenomenological method is somewhat akin to the silk coils that give strength and structure to the web of phenomenology. The third part of the chapter examines three main types of philosophical phenomenology, including transcendental phenomenology, hermeneutic phenomenology and existential phenomenology. Philosophical phenomenology is like the hub of the web of phenomenology; it is the foundation and the origin of all phenomenology.

The next part of the chapter focusses on phenomenology as a way of doing research. Although there are different versions of phenomenological research, only two dominant schools or threads are examined in this section, namely the Utrecht School and the Duquesne School. These two schools are the silk threads that emanate from the hub, or the philosophical insights of phenomenology.

The final part of the chapter is an attempt to hang the web of phenomenology on the 'bridge line' of education. Here I examine the place of phenomenology in educational research, and argue that it has made and continues to make a rich and unique contribution to the discipline of education.

The web of phenomenology: an overview

Phenomenology can be likened to an orb spider's web, consisting of threads, coils, and a hub. The silk spider weaves its web in open areas and threads of dry silk extend from the centre like spokes of a wheel. Coiling lines of silk connect the spokes and serve as a trap. The hub (centre) of any orb web is like the philosophy of phenomenology.

The origins of all phenomenology can be found within the wider philosophical underpinnings. Indeed, all phenomenological studies need to make some acknowledgement of the philosophical traditions that have informed them (van Manen, 1990, p. 7). The individual threads that extend like spokes of a wheel from the hub represent the different approaches that can be used to conduct phenomenological work (for example, more well-known threads include those spun by van Kaam (1966), Langeveld (1968), Vandenberg (1971), Greene (1972), Colaizzi (1978), Giorgi (1985a, 1985b), van Manen (1990) and von Eckartsberg (1998a; 1998b)). Each of these threads has a connection to the philosophical hub at the centre of the web of phenomenology. The silk coils that hold the threads in place are the 'glue' of the web. These coils can be likened to 'the phenomenological method', which consists of four key qualities (i.e. description, reduction, essences and intentionality) common to all types of phenomenology. The coils, then, hold the threads in place and provide support to the web. Without the coils (i.e. the four celebrated themes of phenomenology), the threads (i.e. the various research traditions) have no meaning.

Last but not least, the spider in this scenario is none other than the phenomenologist who spins the phenomenological web. Unlike arachnids who weave webs in order to catch prey, the phenomenologist as spider weaves a web so that he or she can understand the structures of lived experience. An important quest for any phenomenologist is to weave a web that uncovers meaning structures. This chapter is an attempt to disentangle some of the threads and coils of the phenomenological web so that connections between and among tightly woven sheets of understanding will be made known.

Coils of the web: 'the phenomenological method'

Merleau-Ponty, a leading exponent of existentialist phenomenology, wrote in the preface of his book *Phenomenology of Perception* (1962, p. vii) that the question 'what is phenomenology?' had still not been addressed, even though phenomenology was introduced by Husserl at the turn of the century. His response to this question was: 'We shall find in ourselves, and nowhere else, the unity and true meaning of phenomenology'. While this response is not comforting to novice philosophers and/or researchers, his important contribution to phenomenology was an explication of 'the phenomenological method'. At this juncture it is important to note that although Merleau-Ponty (1962) used the term 'phenomenological method', he was not in any way referring to a method or technique for carrying out research. On the contrary, his method provided a way of understanding phenomenology from its philosophical orientation.

'The phenomenological method', according to Merleau-Ponty, embraces four key qualities that are said to be 'celebrated themes' characteristic of phenomenology. Other key writers, such as Natanson (1973, p. 24) and Spiegelberg (1975, p. 57), endorse the four qualities of description, reduction, essences and intentionality as constituting 'the phenomenological method'. These four qualities provide a useful and relatively easy introduction to understanding some of the philosophical underpinnings of phenomenology, and are discussed here.

Description

Phenomenology comes from the Greek *phainomenon*, which means the appearance of things or phenomena (Spinelli, 1989, p. 2). The aim of phenomenology is the description of phenomena, and not the explanation. Phenomena include anything that appears or presents itself, such as emotions, thoughts and physical objects. Phenomenology means describing things as one experiences them, and this means a turning away from science and scientific knowledge and returning to the 'things themselves' (Husserl, 1970a, p. 252). Presuppositions become unnecessary, since the purpose is to investigate the given.

Reduction

According to Husserl, the founding father of phenomenology, there are many different reductions. He describes the epoche, the eidetic or phenomenological reduction, and the transcendental reduction. The differences between these three interrelated reductions will be explored in the discussion that examines Husserl's work. A simple way of viewing the reduction is to think of it as a process where phenomenology requires that taken-for-granted assumptions and presuppositions about phenomena be temporarily suspended or bracketed. The reason for this suspension or bracketing of the phenomena is to ensure that theoretical prejudices do not contaminate the description of the experience (Merleau-Ponty, 1962), and this ensures that 'the things themselves' can be returned to. Husserl's phrase rests on the principle that it is 'living human beings who bring schemas and frameworks into being and not the reverse' (van Manen, 1982, p. 297).

Essences

An essence is simply the core meaning of an individual's experience of any given phenomenon that makes it what it is. The search for essences, essential themes or essential relationships, as they have been called, involves the exploration of phenomena by using the process of free imagination, intuition and reflection. Free variation is used to determine if a particular feature of an essence is essential to it (Spiegelberg, 1975, p. 63). For example, in the case of the essence of learning, a phenomenologist would consider whether or not learning remains an essence without the essential elements of change and development. Spiegelberg (1975, p. 64) further stated:

> Essential insight requires that on the basis of such variation we determine what is essential or necessary and what is merely accidental or contingent.

Once a description is given, the phenomenologist tries to understand the essential structure of the lived experience. Merleau-Ponty (1962, p. xiv) argued that arriving at the essence or essential structure of the phenomenon is not the final step, but is a way by which we can understand the relationships of the experience.

Intentionality

Intentionality is an important concept to consider in Husserl's phenomenology. Intentionality refers to consciousness, and that individuals are always conscious of something (Merleau-Ponty, 1962, p. xviii). Intentionality is the total meaning of the object (for example, idea, process, a person), which is always more than what is given in the perception of a single perspective (Chamberlin, 1974, p. 129). Husserl used the two concepts of noesis and noema to reveal intentionality of consciousness. According to Husserl (Sanders, 1982, p. 354), intentionality refers to the correlation between noema and noesis, both of which lead to the interpretation of an experience. Noema is the objective statement of behaviour or the experience, while noesis is a subjective reflection of the objective statement (Sanders, 1982, p. 357).

A simple example to illustrate noema and noesis is as follows. Twenty teachers attend an in-service seminar conducted by an Education Officer within their region on how to operationalise the Internet in their respective schools. All of the principals listen to the officer explain the advantages of the Internet, how to maximise its usage, and how to use it. As a result of the in-service seminar, it is likely that all of the principals will have different feelings about the Internet and, in some cases, some concerns about this new type of technology. In this example, the noema is the 'what' or the content of the officer's speech that each principal heard, while the noesis is the 'how' or the mode in which each principal heard the speech. The noesis refers to the way in which the principals apprehended the speech, for example whether they felt totally committed to the new technology, their particular concerns or anxieties, and other subjective responses. Together, the noema and the noesis lead each person to interpret an experience in a unique way. As Spinelli (1989, p. 14) stated, no experience can be approached without the presence of both a noematic and noetic focus.

Description, reduction, essences and intentionality are said to bring together common phenomenological themes. The next section is concerned with the hub, or the philosophical underpinnings, of phenomenology.

The hub of phenomenology: philosophical phenomenology

Phenomenology had its origins in the European philosophical tradition. It emerged from the philosophy of Husserl, a late nineteenth-century German mathematician and philosopher (Barritt *et al.*, 1985, p. 19). Since Husserl phenomenology has undergone some expansions and refinement, and today there are a number of schools of thought within it. While Husserl's phenomenology has been labelled 'transcendental', other branches of philosophical phenomenology include existential phenomenology and hermeneutic phenomenology.

Phenomenology is non-dualistic, and therefore does not endorse Descartes' dualism of mind and body, or consciousness and matter. Descartes maintained that there was a distinction between the world of private experience and the world of public objects (Hammond *et al.*, 1991, p. 3). This means that real objects can exist independently of our consciousness. Descartes, like other scientific realists, ascribed importance to 'reality' provided by the physical sciences and regarded subjective experiences as 'appearances'. This position contributed to the privileged situation of science over experience. Phenomenology broke away from this view and sought to develop a philosophy that would give credence to ordinary conscious experience and would not dichotomise appearance from reality. For phenomenologists this separation between appearance and reality, or the separation between the description of objects and the objective external world, is untenable since an experience is always of something (Hammond *et al.*, 1991, p. 2). In some respects Husserl had similar interests to Descartes, as both had the same desire to provide a foundation of human knowledge (Stewart and Mickunas, 1990, p. 21). Husserl's contribution to philosophy was to provide a radical perspective that did not separate mind from matter, but pointed to experience as one is conscious of it as a legitimate type of philosophy. It is to the work of Husserl that attention is now turned.

Transcendental phenomenology: Husserl

Husserl devised both a philosophical phenomenology and a phenomenological psychology; the latter was not only closely related to the former, but also played an important part in the development of his philosophy (Husserl, 1971, p. 82). Husserl was a critic of the then modern psychology because it sought to imitate the physical sciences and rejected the human consciousness, which was, to him, the most important feature of human life.

For Husserl, philosophical phenomenology was the achievement of transcendental subjectivity where the 'absoluteness of conscious existence' could be established (McCall, 1983, p. 56). To Husserl, consciousness was the goal of phenomenology, and consciousness constituted all meaning and being. In simple language, Husserl's main project was to establish a method that would yield absolute essential knowledge or universal unchanging laws of facts (Jennings, 1986, p. 1235).

Understanding reductions is pivotal to understanding Husserl's phenomenology. Husserl used three terms synonymously and interchangeably to describe phenomenological inquiry, namely epoche, bracketing and reduction. Each of these is reviewed briefly, since it is important to understand them in relation to the notion of transcendental phenomenology.

Epoche and bracketing

The term 'epoche' comes originally from the Greek, and it refers to the suspension of beliefs so that the phenomenon can be fully focussed upon and understood. For the epoche to take place, Husserl argued that the natural attitude must be bracketed or suspended. While it is not humanly possible to be completely unbiased and to bracket completely the natural attitude, by being more aware of this process it is possible to try to control it. Bracketing enables the experience to be seen in terms of a new and unconventional perspective. Bracketing or epoche is seen to be the 'essential attitude' of the phenomenologist (Sanders, 1982, p. 355).

Reduction

It is through the epoche that other procedures can then follow. Two of these reductions are the eidetic reduction and the transcendental reduction. It is important to note the complementary relationship that exists between the epoche and the eidetic reduction. As Rogers (1983, pp. 71–72) argued, the epoche brackets the natural attitude and the eidetic reduction makes sense of what remains. Rogers goes on to state:

> What was given before the epoche as a fact can be taken after the epoche as an exemplar of some undetermined but pure possibility. The pure possibility that the object exemplifies is its essence. The eidetic reduction means simply intending an object of consciousness as an exemplar of an essence (or 'eidos').

The eidetic reduction involves the movement from objects as facts to objects as exemplars (essences). In this process, particular features of a phenomenon are reduced or set aside so that note can be taken of 'that which in the phenomenon shows itself as universal' (Carpenter, 1978, p. 38). The method of free variation is used to investigate essences to determine what is secondary and what is unchangeable or essential. According to Husserl, the goal of phenomenological research is to get to the essence of consciousness, and it is the essence that gives meaning to the objects of consciousness.

In order to arrive at pure consciousness or transcendental subjectivity, another reduction is necessary. According to Husserl (Rogers, 1983, p. 73), both the epoche and the eidetic reduction do not address the 'I' but leave it intact, which means that 'consciousness still has common-sense elements'. Hence the next step, known as the transcendental reduction, involves suspending judgment about the existence of everything in the world, including the ego (McCall, 1983, p. 58). In short, Husserl believed it was possible to bracket oneself from one's beliefs in order to get to pure consciousness. Thus in the transcendental reduction the phenomenologist is not concerned with viewing external phenomena but with human consciousness, which determines the meaning and being of everything (McCall, 1983, p. 62). For Husserl, the transcendental ego had a being of its own, distinct from the self.

Husserl's notion of 'transcendental subjectivity' was seen as idealistic (McCall, 1983, pp. 62–63) by his critics, one of whom was Heidegger. Critics felt that his movement away from descriptive phenomenology to a movement that embraced notions of eidetic phenomenology, transcendental consciousness and the exclusion of the natural world was idealistic (Stewart and Mickunas, 1990, p. 46). It is believed that this criticism encouraged him to pursue a different focus, and he did this in his final book, *The Crisis of European Sciences* (Husserl, 1970a). It was in this book that he explicated the notion of the 'life-world' or 'lived-world' (*Lebenswelt*). *Lebenswelt* was seen as the direct link between Husserl's phenomenology and existential philosophy (Stewart and Mickunas, 1990, p. 12).

For Husserl, the life-world is the world we experience in everyday living. It is here that he turned his attention to the experience of the lived-world as the primary task of phenomenology. Related to the lived-world is the concept of 'horizon', which refers to the context in which one experiences things, people or feelings (Stewart and Mickunas, 1990, p. 46). Experiences are not isolated, but take place in particular contexts or horizons. For example, when a school principal experiences professional development, he or she does so in a time and place and in distinction from other objects. The implication in this example is that any research phenomenon needs to be understood within its particular horizon context.

While the *Lebenswelt* marked a shift in Husserl's thinking, both the hermeneutic and existential phenomenologists built on this idea and focussed attention on being-in-the-world. This enabled them to view 'human relationships in the world in terms of the individual's concrete experience' (Stewart and Mickunas, 1990, p. 64).

Hermeneutic phenomenology

The term 'hermeneutic' was first used to refer to interpreting biblical texts and the scriptures. It has been used in more recent times to understand or interpret the world as though it were a text. The hermeneutic phenomenologist needs to put herself or himself in the place of the author of the text in order to comprehend the situation and the person more fully (Barritt *et al.*, 1985, p. 22). According to Nicholson (1997, p. 304), phenomenology became hermeneutical 'when it argued that every form of human awareness is interpretive'. As van Manen states (1990, p. 26), phenomenology includes a descriptive element (phenomenological) as well as an interpretive (hermeneutic) element.

Two prominent philosophers within the hermeneutic tradition were Heidegger and his pupil Gadamer. Heidegger was Husserl's personal assistant at Freiburg University for a time, and he later succeeded him in his professorial post. There is no doubt that his ideas were shaped by Husserl, although he devised his own unique version of phenomenology (McCall, 1983, p. 60). While some authors have labelled Heidegger's work as 'existential phenomenology' (Spinelli, 1989, p. 107), others (Barritt *et al.*, 1985) have posited him in the 'hermeneutic phenomenology' category. According to McCall (1983, p. 66), however, Heidegger rejected all labels and preferred to describe his profession as 'thinking about being'.

Heidegger disagreed with Husserl's notion of transcendental phenomenology, since he believed that subjectivity is not transcendent because it does not illuminate 'being'. Unlike Husserl, Heidegger claimed that being cannot be bracketed or set aside. Being, *sein*, was the capstone of his theory. Heidegger saw that being is present in all persons. He saw that being was more important than consciousness (McCall, 1983, p. 61), and being in the world precedes any thinking about the world. For these reasons, his ideas moved away from Husserl's. Unlike Husserl, he did not see that consciousness constituted the world. For him, people are not apart from the world but are experienced as being-in-the-world. His central question was, 'What does it mean to be?' (Spinelli, 1989, p. 108). He pondered this question throughout his life, but did not come to any definitive solution.

Existential phenomenology

Existentialism, as a movement, had its origins in the nineteenth century. Two prominent spokespersons at that time were Kierkegaard and Nietzsche (Charlesworth, 1975, p. 3). They both rejected socially imposed morality within the western culture, and were concerned with the quest for the meaning of existence for each individual (Spinelli, 1989, p. 107).

It was not until the twentieth century that existentialism

became cemented to the phenomenological method. Ricoeur (Stewart and Mickunas, 1990, pp. 63–64) argued that two streams of thought coalesced to produce existential phenomenology; Husserl's notion of *Lebenswelt*, and the philosophy of Kierkegaard and Nietzsche. Three significant existential phenomenologists who were writing in the twentieth century included Sartre, Merleau-Ponty and Marcel. Rather than focus on the work of any one existential phenomenologist, some of the characteristics of existential phenomenology are explored here.

Existential phenomenology shared with hermeneutic phenomenology a rejection of the notion of Husserl's transcendental phenomenology since it too maintained that the self and consciousness are not separate (Barritt *et al.*, 1985, p. 21). While one of the assumptions of Husserl's transcendental phenomenology was that the world is not already there but is created in consciousness (or constituted in consciousness), Merleau-Ponty took a different view, as he posited that the world already exists and 'consciousness is in dialogue with the world' (Spurling, 1977, p. 10). The existential phrase 'being in the world' means that humans are situated in the world.

Another point of divergence between Husserl and the existential phenomenologists was the issue of 'essence', or ideal meanings or acts of consciousness. The existential phenomenologists emphasised the tension between essence and existence (Rogers, 1983, p. 2) and focussed instead upon human existence and a person's concrete way of living (Spurling 1977, p. 9; Stewart and Mickunas, 1990, p. 65). Hence their phenomenology was known as 'existential', since it was concerned with a person's existence.

In common with the other philosophical phenomenologies, however, existential phenomenology maintained that experience should be a central concern of phenomenology. The way to study human life was to examine experience as found in the everyday world. Central themes of existential phenomenologists included the importance of the body, and of freedom, and the need for authenticity (Rogers, 1983, p. 2). Of these terms, 'authenticity' was a term that both Heidegger and Sartre saw as pivotal to existential phenomenology. For example, Heidegger (Spinelli, 1989, p. 109) argued that human beings adopt an authentic or inauthentic mode of being throughout their lives. To be inauthentic means to conform to prevailing attitudes of the day, and to respond to life experiences in a reactive or passive way. In contrast, to be authentic means that one recognises one's autonomy in the way life is experienced and acknowledges the role of determining one's actions (Spinelli, 1989, p. 109). Put another way:

> The most basic way of being-in-the-world is concern and responsibility for oneself, the world, and for others. Existence is authentic when one freely chooses how he or she will be-in-the-world, but inauthentic when other forces are allowed to shape his or her being-in-the-world. (Mitchell, 1990, p. 74)

Existential phenomenology thus focusses on human existence, and lived experience is the focus point for all philosophical reflection (Compton, 1997, p. 208).

Phenomenological threads: research approaches to phenomenology

The phenomenology of Husserl (1931, 1970a, 1971), Merleau-Ponty (1962) and Heidegger (1962) was written at a theoretical level. Their philosophy was concerned with first person only. None of these philosophers outlined the specific applications of phenomenology to research endeavours; to them, phenomenology was viewed as a pure and theoretical discipline (McDuffie, 1988, p. 52). What we have witnessed over the last 30 years in education and in some of the other disciplines has been the presence of different types of phenomenological writings. For example, two seminal books that used existential phenomenological insights in education were Maxine Greene's (1972) *Teacher as Stranger* and Vandenberg's (1971) *Being and Education*. Both Greene's and Vandenberg's work did not rely on research participants; it was phenomenological writing about education.

Two prominent schools of thought within phenomenology that emerged around 30 years ago were the Utrecht School (which came from the Netherlands) and the Duquesne School (operating out of Duquesne University in Pittsburgh in the United States). Each of these is discussed here, and the work of a key writer within each school is contrasted.

Utrecht School

A key player whose thinking led to the 'Utrecht school' was Martinus Langeveld, whose particular research interest included children's experiences and their ways of perceiving the world. To date, the Utrecht school has developed a broad research programme investigating the life-worlds of children and adolescents (Meyer-Drawe, 1997, p. 159). In recent times the school has taken shape under the influence of Ton Beekman (Meyer-Drawe, 1997, p. 160). Max van Manen, a Dutch phenomenologist who lives in Canada, has connections with this school, and his phenomenological pedagogical work has close ties to the project of the Utrecht school.

Max van Manen – Phenomenology

Van Manen states that his work was influenced by the Dutch movement from the Utrecht school and also the German tradition of 'human science pedagogy'. From Langeveld, who wrote sensitive, reflective studies, he learned about interpretive phenomenological research. From the human science approach he realised the importance of understanding the meaning of human phenomena and the living structures of meaning (van Manen, 1990, p. ix). One of the important contributions he has made to phenomenology has been to identify and discuss questions of method and how to partake in scholarship. His book *Researching Lived Experience* (van Manen, 1990) provides some guidance to those who wish to understand and research human science pedagogy.

As van Manen states, his quest is to understand the phenomena of the lifeworld in order to see the pedagogical significance of situations (van Manen, 1990, p. 2). Thus the outcome of any human science research should be pedagogical competence or, in other words, knowing how to act tactfully (p. 8) and thoughtfully (p. 12). In *The Tact of Teaching* (1991), van Manen provides an original perspective on the practice of teaching as a reflective, sensitive and tactful activity. Tact is described as 'being open to ... [a] child's experience'; 'as attuned to subjectivity'; and 'is governed by insight while relying on feeling' (pp. viii–ix). There is a strong moral dimension to van Manen's work (see, for example, van Manen, 1990, 1991, 1996), and this is evident not only in the particular topics he chooses to research but also in the sensitive and thoughtful ways he writes about pedagogy.

Van Manen's literary writing style has been described as holistic and poetic (Meyer-Drawe, 1997) – holistic because it reveals a depth and insight into the human condition, and poetic because it is sensitive and reflective. It engages the reader in an account of images and sensations that uncover some aspect of human experience. Van Manen states that the reader must be touched by the text.

Van Manen does not offer a step-by-step formula for conducting research, nor does he use terms such as 'data collection' or 'data analysis' in his seminal book *Researching Lived Experience*. Instead he identifies ways of 'investigating experience as we live it' and of making sense of the investigations (for example, 'hermeneutic phenomenological reflection' in Chapter 4 and 'hermeneutic phenomenological writing' in Chapter 5). Regarding ways in which one might investigate experience, he puts forward the following ideas for getting started (pp. 54–74):

- *Use personal experience as a starting point.* This might help provide clues on the nature of the phenomenon.
- *Trace etymological sources.* Doing this might help to put us in touch with the origins of the word and its original meaning.
- *Search for idiomatic phrases.* Such phrases can possess interpretive significance.
- *Obtain experiential descriptions from others.* We borrow other people's experiences in order to come to a deeper understanding of human experience.
- *Protocol writing.* A key way to find out human experiences is to ask participants to write down their experiences.
- *Interview.* This is seen as a way of gathering experiential material. Concrete experiences should be sought.
- *Observe.* A way of entering the life-world of persons is to be a participant and an observer at the same time.
- *Use experiential descriptions in literature.* Literature, poetry, other story forms, biographies, journals, diaries and logs can serve as important sources of possible human experiences.
- *Use art as a source of lived experience.* Objects of art can be used as a source of lived experience.

- *Consult the phenomenological literature.* Material that has already addressed the topic, for example, can be an important source of data.

As can be seen above, his 'thread' of phenomenology departs from Langeveld's (1968) as he includes the experiences of others to help shed light upon the phenomenon. Others' experiences can be sought through interviews, observations and protocol writing. As is evident from the list of ideas above, his approach is one which is literary – art and experiential descriptions in the wider literature (for example, poetry, novels, plays, biographies, and so on) can be used as valid experiences to assist the phenomenological writer.

As for his thoughts on 'data analysis', van Manen does not provide a step-by-step formula for making sense of phenomenological 'data' since phenomenology is 'a method without techniques' (1984, p. 27). He does, however, provide some guidance in terms of reflection and writing (van Manen, 1990, pp. 79–93). For example he states that the phenomenologist should conduct a thematic analysis, which entails determining the themes or 'experiential structures of experience'. Next the phenomenologist should uncover thematic aspects, which means that he/she should identify threads or foci around which the description is facilitated. Another thought he provides is isolating thematic statements, which can be done in three ways; by the holistic approach, the selective approach, and the detailed (or line-by-line) approach. The first of these asks what phrase captures the meaning of the text; the second asks what seems essential or revealing in the text; and in the third, every sentence is examined to see what it reveals about the phenomenon or experience being described. The step of determining essential themes (1990, p. 106) is described by van Manen as quite difficult, as it means determining the universal quality of each theme that makes the phenomenon what it is. Free imagination is a method that he suggests here.

Creating the phenomenological text is the object of the research process (van Manen, 1990, p. 111). Writing is fused into the research activity and is a 'linguistic project' since it makes some aspect of lived experience understandable (van Manen, 1990, pp. 125–126). An important device in his writing is the use of anecdotes or stories. Anecdotes are concrete examples of

insight that are central to writing in the human science discourse. Van Manen claims that 'a powerful narrative anecdote
may (i) compel or recruit our willing attention; (ii) lead us to
reflect; (iii) involve us personally; (iv) transform, touch, shake,
move us' (1996, workshop handout). While anecdotes have no
validity in empirical research, van Manen argues that their place
is assured in phenomenological research.

While van Manen (1984, pp. 26–28) provides some suggestions
for structuring the descriptions of phenomenological writing, he
also points out some pitfalls of phenomenological writing. Some
of these include:

- Failing to be guided by a question
- Losing the sense of wonder of the phenomenological atti-
  tude
- Confusing existential interpretations with perceptions
- Losing touch with experience as we live through it
- Engaging in undisciplined analysis
- Mistreating the text as a depository for private emotions.

To a novice phenomenologist unused to the requirements of
phenomenological research, these pitfalls pose a challenge.
For example, it seems that the final pitfall identified in the list
is one that creates some confusion in phenomenological
research. Phenomenology, strictly speaking, is not autobiographical research, nor is it research that reports on the subjective
perceptions/experiences of individuals. While it can use
experiences from the researcher (for example, see van Manen,
1990), what is essential is the 'phenomenon' itself. For example,
a phenomenological study might be, 'what is love?'. The phenomenologist will draw upon a variety of experiences (for
example, a personal anecdote, anecdotes from others, important
literature such as Fromm's (1957) *The Art of Loving*,
poetry/books/plays, etc. that deal with love, and so on). All of
these experiences will be reflected upon in order to understand
the phenomenon that is 'love'. Thus phenomenological research
is not a depository for private emotions of the happy- or
unhappy-in-love researcher.

Similarly, a phenomenological study does not report on the
emotions of a group of brokenhearted or happy-in-love participants. It is not their subjective experiences that constitute the

project of phenomenology; their anecdotes only serve to cast light upon the phenomenon of love. Phenomenology is sometimes referred to as 'objectivising subjectivity' (Willis, 1996, p. 219). Each phenomenon consists of an objective (noematic) and subjective (noetic) pole, and the subjective pole becomes of interest to the phenomenologist only as a way of understanding the phenomenon itself. Crotty (1996) makes this point loud and clear in his book *Phenomenology and Nursing Research*. He criticises much of the nursing research over the last decade, which claims to use 'a phenomenological approach' but is actually concerned with subjective experiences of participants. He sees that nursing phenomenologists are researching human participants and not human topics or issues (Crotty, 1996, p. 107), unlike mainstream phenomenology, which illuminates phenomena.

In summary, then, we can see that van Manen's version of phenomenology is hermeneutic, literary, and a reflective type of human science approach that is sensitive to lived experience. The next important school of phenomenology which emerged about the same time as did the Utrecht school, was the Duquesne School.

Duquesne School

This other prominent school of thought emerged from the Psychology Department within the Duquesne University. Van Kaam (1966) has been hailed as the founder and originator of the existential phenomenological psychological approach used at this institution (von Eckartsberg, 1998b, p. 24). Since the 1960s, other prominent followers of this tradition have included people such as Giorgi (1971, 1985a, 1985b), Colaizzi (1973) and von Eckartsberg (1998a, 1998b). Each of these psychologists has created his own way of developing an empirical existential phenomenological psychology. The work of Giorgi (1985a, 1985b), which is seen as exemplifying an existential phenomenological approach, is discussed here, along with points of convergence and divergence with van Manen's work.

Amedeo Giorgi – Existential phenomenological psychology

It was stated earlier that Husserl developed a phenomenological philosophy and a phenomenological psychology, each of which

is related to the other. Husserl believed the goal of phenomenological psychology was to apply the phenomenological method
to psychological enquiry. This involved employing the eidetic
reduction, which would provide a description of the nature of
experiences, thereby revealing the 'essences' (McCall, 1983, p.
59). Husserl referred to phenomenological psychology as an
'eidetic science', since the eidetic reduction 'provide[d] the
means of access to the invariant essential structures of the
total sphere of pure mental process' (Husserl, 1971, p. 81).
To make this phenomenological psychology workable, however,
he loosened some of the authoritarian ideas that comprised his
transcendental system (Spinelli, 1989, p. 30). Since Husserl's
time, psychologists have reworked his ideas and blended them
with insights from existential phenomenology to establish psychology as a distinctly human science (Giorgi *et al.*, 1971,
pp. vi–xiii).

Although Husserl attempted to subvert the 'naturalism' that
pervaded psychological thought and practice during the early
part of this century, psychology today is still known as a science
of behaviour, and dominating psychology largely is the positivistic scientific paradigm. Over the last 30 years, however, a
group of psychologists (van Kaam, 1966; Colaizzi, 1978; Giorgi,
1971; Giorgi *et al.*, 1971) asserted that psychology had much to
gain by being informed from a phenomenological approach. The
result was existential phenomenological psychology as an alternative (Valle and King, 1978; Valle *et al.*, 1989; Valle, 1998).

Giorgi (1971) argued that psychology must develop its own
methods and procedures that do not rely upon the natural sciences. He thus turned to the theoretical insights of existential
phenomenological philosophy, and endeavoured to apply these
to the study of psychology. Due to the complexity of applying
the phenomenological method to concrete research, Giorgi trans-
lated the phenomenological perspective into a scientific methodology. He felt this was necessary because the 'phenomenological
method' as articulated by Merleau-Ponty (1962) and Spiegelberg
(1975) was written at a theoretical level and thus was ambiguous
for concrete research.

Giorgi (1985a, pp. 47–52) turned to Merleau-Ponty's four criteria of the phenomenological method, and expressed these in a
way that is helpful for phenomenological psychology. These four
themes are explored here.

1 *Description*. The first and most crucial point Giorgi made is that when one moves from philosophy to psychology, one moves from self to others. In phenomenological psychology the descriptions come from the participants, as it is their experiences that are sought. He argued that this move is non-phenomenological in the true sense because phenomenology strictly interpreted depends on self-evidence and the self (following Husserl's claims).

2 *Reduction*. In phenomenological philosophy, philosophers usually begin by bracketing their presuppositions before embarking upon the description. In phenomenological psychological research, however, this is not possible. Participants describe phenomena within the natural attitude. The point Giorgi made here is that naive descriptions are accepted by participants, and the reduction occurs when the researcher begins to analyse the descriptions. He argued that a transcendental reduction cannot take place within phenomenological psychology, since this would mean that both the object of the experience and the acts of the experience would be reduced. In phenomenological psychology only a partial reduction occurs, which means the object pole (noema) is reduced while the subject pole (noesis) is not. To illustrate this, he gives the example of a client who describes an early memory to his therapist. While the therapist knows from other sources that this memory is false, he nevertheless lets the client continue his elaboration. The therapist or researcher operating within the phenomenological psychological orientation would understand that the consciousness of the subject is a real process because it is this mode of human consciousness that is of interest to him or her. Within the analysis, the therapist or researcher would perform a reduction on the object (the noema).

3 *Essences*. Giorgi argued that the search for essences in phenomenological psychology is similar to the search for essences within phenomenology. Free variation is still used to uncover the 'invariants' of the phenomenon. The main difference is that in phenomenological philosophy the philosopher seeks universal invariants, while in phenomenological psychology the psychologist seeks general essences that are context related, rather than universal. The essences or structures that are uncovered in the descriptions are general,

because the meanings arrived at are more able to change due to their relationship to contexts or situations.

4   *Intentionality.* This final criterion pertaining to phenomenological philosophy is the notion of intentionality. Just as consciousness is always intended toward an object, in psychology behaviour is seen as intentional and always directed towards a situation. Unlike pure consciousness, the body is given credence, and behavioural descriptions involve the body. From the points above, it is evident that Giorgi modified the general criteria of the phenomenological method articulated by Merleau-Ponty, in order to make it acceptable to psychology.

Giorgi's work has been used in a variety of psychological circles, and has concentrated on clinical, social psychological, and systematic psychological inquiries (Giorgi *et al.*, 1971, p. xii). His methodology has also been used in wider circles, such as education and nursing. Similarly to van Manen, a source of data used by Giorgi is the interview. Giorgi's work relies largely on interviews where he asks participants (this might be one or many) to write or speak about a specific experience of a phenomenon. This is where the similarity ends, as followers of phenomenological psychological research tend not to use other types of experiential data as suggested by van Manen. An exception is a new type of methodology recently developed from existential phenomenological psychology, termed 'hermeneutic phenomenological psychology', advocated by writers such as von Eckartsberg (1998b). Within this approach a wider data base is used for analysis – for example, myths, stories, art and so on. This methodology does not claim to be 'empirical'.

The researcher following the existential phenomenological psychological approach advocated by Giorgi reflects upon the descriptions provided by participants and endeavours to explicate the meaning of the phenomenon being studied in a psychologically significant way. Giorgi (1985b, pp. 11–19) outlines four key steps to follow when analysing data utilising a phenomenological psychological approach:

1   *Reading of the entire description to get a sense of the whole statement.* This involves the researcher reading and re-reading the narratives from the transcribed tape recordings or

written protocols. These narratives describe the human experiences and consciousness of the participants in the study.

2   *Discrimination of meaning units within a psychological perspective and focussed on the phenomenon being researched.* This step involves the researcher breaking down the text into more manageable units and discriminating 'meaning units' with a focus on the phenomenon (Giorgi, 1985b, p. 11). A meaning unit is simply made up of words or phrases that clearly express a meaning that distinguishes the meaning unit from other meaning units. At this stage, the subject's language is not altered in any way.

3   *Transformation of participant's everyday expressions into psychological language with emphasis on the phenomenon being investigated.* For these transformations to be arrived at, the process of reflection and imaginative variation needs to occur. It is here that the researcher asks: 'What is essential in this meaning unit?'. Imaginative variation is the process that the researcher employs to determine what is essential and what is accidental.

4   *Synthesis of transformed meaning units into a consistent statement of the structure of learning. This includes: (4a) a synthesis of situated structural descriptions and (4b) a synthesis of general structural descriptions.* Here the researcher synthesises the insights within the meaning units into a consistent description of the structure of the event. To arrive at a general structural description involves synthesising each of the participant's specific structural descriptions into a general structural description that represents 'the most general meaning of the phenomena' (Giorgi, 1985b, p. 20). As Giorgi stated, it is necessary that all of the meaning units are implicitly contained in this general structure. This final stage (4b) is very important in a phenomenological study because it recognises the commonalities across the sample of participants' experience of the phenomena. The finding of a phenomenological psychological study is the general structural description or statement that is a synthesis of each of the subject's specific statements.

Some points of convergence and divergence can be identified between van Manen's and Giorgi's approaches to phenomenology. As some of them have already been alluded to, only three issues are dealt with now. The first issue is that of the empirical nature of phenomenology. Van Manen's version of phenomenology is not an empirical analytic science (1990, p. 21), for he states that phenomenology 'is not inductively empirically derived'. In contrast, the work of Giorgi (1985a, 1985b) is empirical as it bases itself on factual data that are collected for the purpose of examination and explication (von Eckartsberg, 1998, p. 16). Furthermore, researchers within the phenomenological psychological method are explicit about the research design of their investigation, and the data collection and analysis steps are well-known (von Eckartsberg, 1998, p. 16). While Giorgi's steps for analysis are clearly identified, van Manen maintains that phenomenological research is not a step-by-step process; it is neither structured nor procedural.

The second issue concerns imaginative variation. Both van Manen and Giorgi see that imaginative variation is an important process that allows the researcher to discover which aspects or qualities of a phenomenon are essential and which are incidental. For example, the question, 'what is essential in this meaning unit?' is one that Giorgi asks. Similarly, van Manen asks, 'is this phenomenon still the same if we imaginatively change or delete this theme from the phenomenon?'.

Hanging the web of phenomenology on the bridge line of education

An important thread that holds a spider's web is the bridge line. In this final part of the chapter, I fasten the web of phenomenology to the bridge line of education and attempt to examine the contribution phenomenology has made and continues to make to educational research.

There has been a strong move to an interpretive or qualitative approach in educational research since the 1960s (Burns, 1994, p. 2), and, as argued previously, phenomenology has been viewed as having a strong connection with the assumptions underpinning qualitative research. In philosophy it emerged in the late nineteenth century as a reaction against the then dominant scientific view of the world, and in education in the twentieth century it emerged as a challenge to the behaviouristic psychological agenda (Maykut and Morehouse, 1994). As was stated previously, phenomenological writing became prominent in the

1960s and 1970s and the phenomenological writers at that time made a valuable contribution to understanding educational phenomena as well as providing an alternative view.

Van Manen argues that in recent years there has been a resurgence of the phenomenological tradition in the human sciences (van Manen, 1990). While this may be so, phenomenological research remains on the periphery within educational qualitative research. For example, Bartlett (1994, pp. 207–208) does not include phenomenology as one of the growing areas of qualitative research in Australia. He does note, however, that some of the more popular types of qualitative research include participatory action research, critical education science, qualitative educational sociology (i.e. post-modern and post-structuralist insights), case study methods, policy analysis and feminist research. That Bartlett does not mention phenomenological research is not surprising, given its limited use in education compared with more popular types of qualitative research.

Conclusion

In this chapter I have attempted to examine two prominent schools (one European, the other American) and two prominent writers from those schools that have endorsed a phenomenological approach to researching lived experience. I believe that Max van Manen's contribution to phenomenology has been felt not only in advancing the methodology of phenomenology, but also in the strong moral message underscored in his work, which reminds us of our humanness in everyday life. Giorgi's contribution, like that of his contemporaries (for example, van Kaam, 1966; Colaizzi, 1978; von Eckartsberg, 1998a, 1998b), has been to give psychology a human face with a meaningful character of lived experience. Furthermore, his project to use phenomenological insights for psychology (by casting a thread from the hub of phenomenology) has meant the inclusion of an important approach for doing existential phenomenological psychological research.

The search for meaning and understanding is part of the search of being and becoming more human. Phenomenology shares this search for understanding the problems of human existence. Perhaps part of our quest as weavers of phenomenological webs is to help others see that within the complex orb web lie beautiful and connected threads and coils that extend from the hub or the origins of phenomenological thought.

Bibliography

Barritt, L., Beekman, T., Bleeker, H. and Mulderij, K. (1985) *Researching Educational Practice*. North Dakota Study Group on Evaluation. Grand Forks: North Dakota University (microfiche).

Bartlett, L. (1994) Qualitative research in Australia. *Qualitative Studies in Education* 7(3): 207–225.

Burns, R. (1994) *Introduction to Research Methods*. London: Longman Cheshire.

Carpenter, P. (1978) The phenomenology of Edmund Husserl. *Forum of Education* 37(I): 32–44.

Chamberlin, J. (1974) Phenomenological methodology and understanding education. *In*: D. Denton (ed.), *Existentialism and Phenomenology in Education*, pp. 119–137. Columbia: Teachers College Press.

Charlesworth, M. (1975) *The Existentialists and Jean-Paul Sartre*. St Lucia, Queensland: University of Queensland Press.

Colaizzi, P. F. (1978) Psychological research as the phenomenologist views it'. *In*: R. S. Valle and M. King (eds), *Existential Phenomenological Alternatives for Psychology*, pp. 48–71. New York, NY: Oxford University Press.

Compton, J. L. (1997) Existential phenomenology. *In*: L. Embree (ed.), *Encyclopedia of Phenomenology*, pp. 205–209. Dordrecht: Kluwer Academic Publishers.

Crotty, M. (1996) *Phenomenology and Nursing Research*. South Melbourne: Churchill Livingstone.

Embree, L. and Mohanty, J. N. (1997) Introduction. *In*: L. Embree (ed.), *Encyclopedia of Phenomenology*, pp. 1–10, Dordrecht: Kluwer Academic Publishers.

Fromm, E. (1957) *The Art of Loving*. London: Allen and Unwin.

Giorgi, A. (1971) Phenomenology and experimental psychology. *In*: A. Giorgi, W. F. Fischer and R. Von Eckartsberg (eds), *Phenomenological Psychology: Volume 1*, pp. 6–16. Pittsburgh, PA: Duquesne University Press and Humanities Press.

Giorgi, A. (1985a) Phenomenological psychology of learning and the verbal tradition. *In*: A. Giorgi (ed.), *Phenomenology and Psychological Research*, pp. 23–85. Pittsburgh, PA: Duquesne University Press.

Giorgi, A. (1985b) Sketch of a psychological phenomenological method.

In: A. Giorgi (ed.), *Phenomenology and Psychological Research*, pp. 3–21. Pittsburgh, PA: Duquesne University Press.

Giorgi, A., Fischer, W. F. and von Eckartsberg, R. (eds.) (1971) *Duquesne Studies in Phenomenological Psychology: Volume 1*. Pittsburgh, PA: Duquesne University Press and Humanities Press.

Greene, M. (1972) *Teacher as Stranger*. Belmont, CA: Wadsworth.

Hammond, M., Howarth, J. and Keat, R. (1991) *Understanding Phenomenology*. Oxford: Blackwell.

Heidegger, M. (1962) *Being and Time*. Oxford: Basil Blackwell.

Husserl, E. (1931) *Ideas: General Introduction to Pure Phenomenology*. London: George Allen and Unwin Ltd.

Husserl, E. (1970a) *The Crisis of European Sciences and Transcendental Phenomenology: An Introduction to Phenomenological Philosophy*. Evanston, WY: Northwestern University Press.

Husserl, E. (1970b) *Logical Investigations, Vol. 1*. New York, NY: Humanities Press.

Husserl, E. (1971) Phenomenology: Edmund Husserl's article for the Encyclopaedia Britannica 1927: new complete translation by R. E. Palmer. *The British Society for Phenomenology* 2(2): 77–90.

Jennings, J. L. (1986) Husserl revisited: the forgotten distinction between psychology and phenomenology. *American Psychologist* 41(11): 1231–1240.

Langeveld, M. J. (1968) *Studien Zur Anthropologie des Kindes*. Tubingen: Max Niemeyer.

Maykut, P. M. and Morehouse, R. (1994) *Beginning Qualitative Research: a Philosophic and Practical Guide*. London: Falmer Press.

McCall, R. J. (1983) *Phenomenological Psychology: An Introduction*. Wisconsin: The University of Wisconsin Press.

McDuffie, K. (1988) Phenomenology and Australian education. Unpublished MA Thesis, Monash University, Australia.

Merleau-Ponty, M. (1962) *The Phenomenology of Perception*. London: Routledge and Kegan Paul.

Merriam, S. B. and Simpson, E. L. (1984) *A Guide to Research for Educators and Trainers of Adults*. Malabar, FL: Robert E. Krieger Publishing.

Meyer-Drawe, K. (1997) Education. *In*: L. Embree (ed.), *Encyclopedia of Phenomenology*, pp. 157–162. Dordrecht: Kluwer Academic Publishers.

Mitchell, J. G. (1990) *Revisioning Educational Leadership: A Phenomenological Approach*. New York, NY: Garland Publishing Inc.

Natanson, M. (ed.) (1973) *Phenomenology and the Social Sciences, Vol. 1*. Evanston, WY: Northwestern University Press.

Nicholson, G. (1997) Hermeneutical phenomenology. *In*: L. Embree (ed.), *Encyclopedia of Phenomenology*, pp. 304–308. Dordrecht: Kluwer Academic Publishers.

Patton, M. Q. (1990) *Qualitative Evaluation and Research Methods*. Newbury Park, CA: Sage.

Rogers, M. F. (1983) *Sociology, Ethnomethodology, and Experience: a Phenomenological Critique*. Cambridge: Cambridge University Press.

Sanders, P. (1982) Phenomenology: a new way of viewing organisational research. *Academy of Management Review* 7(3): 353–360.

Spiegelberg, H. (1975) *Doing Phenomenology: Essays on and in Phenomenology*. The Hague: Martin Nijhoff.

Spinelli, E. (1989) *The Interpreted World: An Introduction to Phenomenological Psychology*. London: Sage.

Spurling, L. (1977) *Phenomenology and the Social World: The Philosophy of Merleau-Ponty and its Relation to the Social Sciences*. London: Routledge and Kegan Paul.

Stewart, D. and Mickunas, A. (1990) *Exploring Phenomenology: a Guide to the Field and its Literature*. Athens, OH: Ohio University Press.

Valle, R. (ed.) (1998) *Phenomenological Inquiry in Psychology: Existential and Transpersonal Dimensions*. New York, NY: Plenum Press.

Valle, R. S. and King, M. (eds) (1978) *Existential–Phenomenological Alternatives for Psychology*. New York, NY: Oxford University Press.

Valle, R. S., King, M. and Halling, S. (1989) An introduction to existential-phenomenological thought in psychology. *In*: R. S. Valle and S. Halling (eds), *Existential–Phenomenological Alternatives for Psychology*, pp. 3–16. New York, NY: Plenum Press.

Vandenberg, D. (1971) *Being and Education*. Englewood Cliffs, NJ: Prentice Hall.

van Kaam, A. (1966) *Existential Foundations for Psychology*. New York, NY: Appelton Century Crofts.

van Manen, M. (1982) Phenomenological pedagogy. *Curriculum Inquiry* 12(3): 283–299.

van Manen, M. (1984) *Doing Phenomenological Research and Writing: An Introduction*. Monograph No. 7. Department of Secondary Education, Faculty of Education, University of Alberta, Publication Services.

van Manen, M. (1990) *Researching Lived Experience: Human Science for an Action Sensitive Pedagogy*. Ontario: University of Western Ontario, Althouse Press.

van Manen, M. (1991) *The Tact of Teaching: The Meaning of Pedagogical Thoughtfulness*. Albany, NY: State University of New York Press.

van Manen, M. (1996) *The Gnostic and Pathic Hand*. Public Lecture, Monash University Australia, Proceedings of Asian Pacific Health Sciences Conference, January.

von Eckartsberg, R. (1998a) Introducing existential–phenomenological psychology. *In*: R. Valle (ed.), *Phenomenological Inquiry in Psychology: Existential and Transpersonal Dimensions*, pp. 3–20. New York, NY: Plenum Press.

von Eckartsberg (1998b) Existential–phenomenological research. *In*:
    R. Valle (ed.), *Phenomenological Inquiry in Psychology: Existential
    and Transpersonal Dimensions,* pp. 21–61. New York, NY: Plenum
    Press.
Willis, P. (1996) Representation and interpretation in phenomenological
    research. *In*: P. Willis and B. Neville (eds), *Qualitative Research Practice
    in Adult Education,* pp. 215–250. Ringwood, Victoria: David Lovell
    Publishing

Chapter 5

Methodological framings for a policy trajectory study

Lesley Vidovich

Introduction

'Quality' was a catchcry of the 1990s across both private and public sectors globally, and education was no exception. 'Quality' policies have become important mechanisms for increasing educational accountability to external stakeholders, and, arguably, such policies represent an ideological shift privileging economic rationales in education policy making. This chapter focusses on an analysis of the first 'quality' policy in Australian higher education as it evolved during the 1990s, within a context of globalisation. Given the high cost of the quality audits (real and opportunity costs of university staff time), the high profile of the ensuing league tables and debate in the media, and the implications for both universities and academics adjusting to a more competitive climate, this quality policy warranted close scrutiny. Further, given the ongoing evolution of 'quality' policy in Australian higher education, and the development of parallel (similar but different) quality policies in the university sectors of many other countries across the globe, the type of research reported in this chapter should be of interest well beyond the specifics of the policy analysis featured here.

A central finding of the study to which this chapter relates was that the operation of the Australian higher education quality policy processes of the 1990s provided an example *par excellence* of the mechanism of 'steering at a distance'. On the one hand the policy parameters were clearly set by ministerial guidelines, but on the other hand the minutiae of the programme were shaped by the national Committee for Quality Assurance in Higher Education (CQAHE) (which conducted the quality audits of universities) and institutional managers in universities. However, 'room for manoeuvre' at the micro-level of this policy process had definite boundaries. Although there was some variation in policy practices at different university sites, especially evident in different types of universities, the 'bigger picture' effect was clearly to increase government control of higher education, on the rationale of serving 'the national interest'.

Another major conclusion of the study was that the quality policy under investigation was a 'clever' strategy employed by a Commonwealth government aiming to create a 'clever' country to enhance its position in the global marketplace. Two particular features of the Australian context were relevant to understanding the nature of this 'clever' policy. The first feature was the federal structure, which sees the Commonwealth government occupying a relatively powerful financial position in higher education, enabling it to dictate policy for universities using financial levers, with very little resistance. During the late 1980s the federal minister responsible for higher education had signalled enhanced control of higher education by the government using accountability mechanisms such as quantitative performance indicators, but by the early 1990s there was growing sector criticism of this 'coercive federalism' and the interventionist style of the government. Thus, quality policy provided a vehicle for the government apparently to 'back off' in respect of university autonomy, but in essence the effect was to tighten steerage using incentives of money and status, as the country's 37 universities were all wanting to emerge at the top of the quality league tables.

The second feature of the Australian context relevant to understanding the 'clever' strategy of quality policy in Australian higher education was the fact that the Labour Party in government was wanting to retain some semblance of a social democratic orientation, in contrast to countries such as the United Kingdom and United States, where more fully developed market ideologies were evident under Conservative governments. As a Labour government was unlikely to want to be associated with full privatisation, it could opt instead for greater corporatisation of government enterprises and the use of quasi-markets to achieve the desired efficiency and effectiveness. Quality league tables provided such a quasi-market mechanism, which would sit more comfortably with Labour ideology.

Quality policy was also 'clever' because the concept of 'quality' itself has a chameleon character of multiple discourses that might satisfy 'some of the people most of the time', thereby reducing potential resistance from the sector. In particular, there was slippage in the policy discourses between the notion of 'excellence', which has a traditional presence in universities, with the conceptualisation of quality as accountability to external stakeholders. Quality policy led a metamorphosis of accountability in Australian higher education from professional and democratic forms towards managerial and market forms. Therefore, in a number of significant ways quality policy was well adapted to its time and place in transforming Australian higher education to serve 'the national interest' – as defined by government.

This chapter is concerned with reflections on the methods used to conduct the analysis of the particular quality policy under investigation in Australian higher education. The chapter consists of three main sections. First, the aim and research questions are delineated, as they clearly guided the data collection and analysis. Second, the theoretical and methodological frameworks are overviewed, as theory and methods were closely interwoven in this study: theory informed methods, which again informed theory. This approach is consistent with that of LeCompte and Preissle (1993), Ball (1994a) and Ozga and Gewirtz (1994), who have urged greater efforts with theory building alongside empirical studies. The third and longest section of this chapter reflects on the specifics of the data gathering and analysis, with separate discussions of documentary and interview data. As interview data were the primary focus, and they also rendered what was most unique about this study, more time was spent on data gathering and analysis from interviews than from documents. Ultimately, there is some potential extrapolation to other instances of education policy analysis, and to qualitative research methods generally.

Aim and research questions

The principal aim of the study was to analyse Australian higher education's quality policy processes of the 1990s. Five groups of specific research questions were derived from the general aim. The research questions, presented below, were designed around the three contexts of 'influence', 'policy text production' and 'practice' at four different levels (macro, intermediate, micro and mini-micro) of the quality policy process under investigation. The research questions were:

1   *Context of influence*
    • What were the factors influencing the initiation of Australia's higher education quality policy during the 1990s? (macro, intermediate and micro perceptions)
2   *Context of policy text production*
    • How was the policy text constructed by the minister and Higher Education Council? (macro processes)
    • How did the Committee for Quality Assurance in Higher Education (CQAHE) reconstruct the policy text? (intermediate processes)
    • How did universities reconstruct the policy text? (micro processes)
3   *Context of practice (effects)*
    • Quality: What were the effects of the quality policy on practices both within universities and across the higher education sector? (intermediate and micro perceptions)
    • Accountability: What were the effects of the umbrella policy domain of accountability on practices both within universities and across the higher education sector? *(mini-micro perceptions)*
4   *Synthesising a policy trajectory*
    • Can a policy trajectory be synthesised that links the various contexts and levels of this policy process, and allows for the 'messy realities' of a non-linear policy process?
5   *Evaluating the effectiveness of the theoretical tools*
    • How useful was the theoretical concept of a policy trajectory, including the modifications made for the analysis of the particular Australian higher education quality policy investigated in this study?

It is important to highlight that this study conceptualised the policy process as continuous throughout different levels and contexts. However, the separation between the different components of the policy process was artificially imposed to facilitate analysis. Documents and interviews were the principal data sources used to research the above questions, although at each context and level specific methods of data collection and analysis were modified to adapt to the changing place and time. Analysis of data obtained at any one level was often fed back into the data collection at another level of the trajectory, as good ethnographic practice suggests (Bowe et al., 1992). Given the close interweaving of theory and methods, there is a need briefly to outline the theoretical and methodological frameworks before proceeding.

The theoretical and methodological frameworks

The study was located within the general domains of policy sociology (Ozga, 1987; Ball, 1990; Raab, 1994a) and critical policy analysis (Prunty, 1985; Codd, 1988; Ball, 1994b, 1997; Troyna, 1994; Taylor, 1997). The conceptual toolboxes employed revolve around two approaches to education policy analysis, which are often presented in the literature as binary opposites. On the one hand there is the 'state control' approach, represented by Roger Dale (1989), and on the other hand there is the 'policy cycle' conception of the policy process represented by the work of Stephen Ball (1994b). Debates on the relative merits of these positions have featured strongly in the policy literature in the last decade (Lingard, 1993; Troyna, 1994; Taylor, 1997). The 'state control' position advocates that state institutions and apparatuses form a powerful policy elite that not only attempts to maintain a tight control over public policy generally, including education, but is also largely successful in imposing a policy agenda on practitioners. By contrast, the 'policy cycle' view is that there has not been a total exclusion of practitioners from the policy process, and that the focus should be on the active interpretation and agency by micro-political actors to include, according to Bowe et al. (1992, p. 13), 'resistance, accommodations, subterfuge and conformity within and between arenas of practice and the plotting of clashes and mismatches between contending discourses at work in these arenas'. Bowe et al. proposed a continuous policy cycle or policy trajectory to allow for the recontextualisation of policy throughout the whole process. They distinguished the three primary policy contexts of 'influence' (where interest groups struggle over construction of policy discourses), 'policy text production' (where texts represent policy, although they may contain inconsistencies and contradictions), and 'practice' (where policy is subject to interpretation and recreation). Each of these three contexts has multiple arenas of action (both public and private), and each involves struggles.

The approach in this study was to reject both a binary divide between 'state control' and 'policy cycle' perspectives, and a simplistic separation of policy formulation and implementation. The literature points to a growing dissatisfaction with such dichotomies and a greater preparedness to find some middle ground. For example, Fitz and Halpin (1994a) supported a balanced approach between the centre's power to disseminate policy and the capacity of practitioners to interpret policies rather than simply execute them. Gale (1994) argued for retaining both the coherence of structural analysis and the complexity of post-structuralist accounts of policy. He maintained that 'the micro level of the state is not without structure, nor the macro level without agency, but micro-politics and political constraints are evident in both' (p. 3).

The notion of a policy trajectory (Bowe et al., 1992; Ball, 1994b) formed the foundation of the theoretical framework used in this study, and four different levels of the trajectory were differentiated: macro, intermediate, micro and mini-micro levels. Gillborn (1994) has emphasised the importance of building a more sophisticated view of how macro changes are reconstructed at the micro level, and Taylor (1997) has more recently observed a general agreement among policy analysts that both **macro** and **micro** levels need to be taken into account. For Australia's higher education quality policy of the 1990s, at the *macro* level of policy text production were the minister and the Higher Education Council. Together they provided the broad parameters of the policy in 1991 and 1992, and then continued to reconstruct quality policy text throughout the 1990s. At the *intermediate* level, the Committee for Quality Assurance in Higher Education (CQAHE) was a ministerial committee created to refine the policy text and conduct quality reviews of universities between 1993 and 1995. The sites of policy practice in individual universities were subdivided into *micro* (institutional managers) and *mini-micro* (grassroots academics) levels of the trajectory. The logic of the separation of the two groups within universities was the growing reference to a gap between the perspectives of managers and grassroots academics within the increasingly corporate management style of university governance in Australia (Bessant, 1995; Illing, 1998).

A number of modifications were made to Ball's conceptualisation of a policy trajectory to take into account both criticisms of that approach and the nature of the particular policy under investigation. The first modification was to extend the terrain from within an individual nation state to the global context, as suggested by Lingard (1996) and later by Ball himself (1997). Globalisation is an increasingly documented phenomenon, and therefore its potential effect on education policy processes must be examined. The second modification was to incorporate both state-centred constraint and micro-political agency into the policy trajectory. The approach was 'state centred', to emphasise the government's central role in the quality policy, but not 'state controlled', which implies a top-down implementation model (Raab, 1994b). Thus the micro-political complexities and 'messiness' of quality policy processes were examined (especially at the level of individual universities, which have different historical, geographical, cultural and social contexts), although the 'bigger picture' (Ozga, 1990) was kept in mind throughout. The third modification to the policy trajectory was explicitly to highlight the interlinkages between different levels and contexts of the policy process, as suggested by Taylor (1997). For example, data from the intermediate level were compared and contrasted with that from the micro level, and then the mini-micro level. Possible avenues and mechanisms for feedback from micro-level policy practices to both the contexts of influence and policy text production at the macro level were also explored.

This study called for a qualitative approach to investigate in depth the complexity and the messiness of the quality policy processes in Australian higher education. Qualitative research places a greater emphasis on inductive, generative, constructive and subjective processes than on deductive, verificative, enumerative and objective processes (Goetz and LeCompte, 1984). The importance given to context in qualitative research (Patton, 1990; Cassell and Symon, 1994) was most appropriate to this study where the existence of context-specific variations in the quality policy process were of particular interest. Qualitative researchers 'usually work with small samples of people nested in their contexts' (Miles and Huberman, 1994, p. 27).

Following the stance by Patton (1990) that 'the qualitative

researcher has an obligation to be methodical in reporting sufficient details of data collection and the process of analysis to
permit others to judge the quality of the resulting product' (p.
402), the dynamics of data collection and analysis are presented
here. Further, responding to calls by certain prominent policy
sociologists for methodological reflexivity (Fitz and Halpin,
1994b; Troyna, 1994; Walford, 1994a; Batteson & Ball, 1995),
some of the problematic, serendipitous and possibly less comfortable aspects of the methods used are also included. Jordan
and Yeomans (1995) have emphasised that reflexivity turns the
focus on both the researcher and the research act as part of the
social world being investigated, and therefore it involves a
dialectic between the researcher, the research process and the
research product. Tritter (1995) has argued that reflexivity
involves researchers being aware of their own responses and
repeating accounts back to respondents to facilitate the construction of a joint account of the phenomenon being researched, both
of which were integral to this study.

Debates about the reliability and validity of qualitative
research have raged, although the arguments will not be
rehearsed here. Reliability is the extent to which a study can be
replicated, whereas internal validity is the extent to which
researchers are observing/measuring what they think they are
observing/measuring, and external validity is the extent to
which the findings are applicable to other groups (LeCompte
and Preissle, 1993). Some qualitative researchers choose not to
use these terms. For example, Goetz and LeCompte (1984) talked
about the generalisation of the findings, which can be
approached through comparability and translatability. They
believed that comparability is facilitated by the use of standard
terminology and analytical frames, as well as clear delineation of
the group studied. Translatability assumes that methods and
analytical categories as well as characteristics of the phenomena
and groups are explicitly identified. Other qualitative
researchers, such as Miles and Huberman (1994), have proposed
alternative terms that sit in parallel with reliability and validity.
They paired reliability with dependability and auditibility;
internal validity with credibility and authenticity; and external
validity with transferability and fittingness. More frequently,
though, they talked in general terms about ensuring the 'good-
ness' of qualitative research.

Triangulation as a means of enhancing reliability and validity features frequently in the qualitative methodology literature. It involves cross-checking or cross-referencing the data (LeCompte and Preissle, 1993; Batteson and Ball, 1995) by combining different perceptions of the same event to provide a more robust and holistic picture (Tritter, 1995). Various types of triangulation have been distinguished, depending upon whether it is achieved through multiple methods, sources, researchers, theories and/or data types (Patton, 1990; Miles and Huberman, 1994). Most of these approaches to triangulation were employed in this study, with, for example, the use of different data collection methods within each level in the policy trajectory and different individual sources within each method. Triangulation was also possible between different levels of the trajectory when the same interview questions were asked, although the aim was certainly not always to build a single coherent picture but often to highlight differences for interpretation.

Data gathering and analysis

Documentary data

Documents formed the main source of data for the analysis of the macro level of the quality policy trajectory. Furthermore, at the lower levels of the trajectory documents provided valuable information in preparing for interviews and also for triangulating with interview data.

Walford (1994a, p. 229) has emphasised that 'documentary evidence cannot simply be understood at face value. The story behind the production of each document needs to be probed and analysed'. Similarly, May (1993) drew attention to the need to examine factors surrounding the process of a document's production as well as its social context because documents both reflect and construct a social reality. In this study, both the global and Australian contexts within which relevant documents were produced was overviewed at the outset. Furthermore, the context of specific documents produced at the different levels of the quality policy trajectory was incorporated into each part of the ongoing analysis.

A discourse analysis approach to documentary data sources is increasingly common. In the 1980s, Codd (1988) argued for the use of theories of discourse in analysing education policy documents as an alternative to more traditional technical-empiricist approaches. He described discourse analysis as a type of textual deconstruction that enables the relationship between language and ideology to be examined critically. He emphasised that discourse analysis should begin with explicit acknowledgement of the context of the text and then proceed to reveal all of the text's ideological ambiguities, distortions and absences. Taylor (1997) referred to the influence of Codd's work in the education policy arena in Australia and New Zealand, and similarly she argued that a discourse theory approach provides a valuable tool for critical policy analysis to highlight values and tease out competing discourses and contradictions. She also emphasised the importance of providing a context for the text.

Although discourse analysis is defined in various ways, it frequently refers to an examination of the way in which language, as social practice, produces and reproduces social structures (Gilbert and Low, 1994; Marshall, 1994; Kamler et al., 1997; Skillington, 1997). For example, Hajer (1995, p. 60) has defined discourse as 'a specific ensemble of ideas, concepts, and categorisations that is produced, reproduced, and transformed in a particular set of practices and through which meaning is given to physical and social realities'. Power is a central concept in the notion of discourse, and the aim of discourse analysis is to reveal the inherent power relations. As Ball (1994a, p. 108) has explained, 'discourses embody and produce relations of power through the promotion of certain subjectivities and meaning systems over others'. A form of discourse analysis was used in this study to tease out the competing and contradictory discourses of quality in key policy documents at the macro level. It was not intended as a fine-grained discourse analysis, but it had the intention of revealing the struggles over the meaning of the text and the resultant internal contradictions in the policy.

In terms of the specific documents examined in this study, at the macro level a policy ensemble or collection of related policies (Ball, 1994b) produced by the minister responsible for higher education and the Higher Education Council were analysed for the way in which the inherent discourses attempted to construct a particular version of quality policy that privileged certain voices over others. Key documents were a ministerial level policy statement (Baldwin, 1991) and budget statement

(Vanstone, 1996) and a series of Higher Education Council discussion papers and final reports to ministers between 1992 and 1998. Most of these documents were readily available, as they were published by the Australian Government Publishing Service and thus were in the public domain. The Vanstone budget statement was on the World Wide Web within minutes of being released.

At the intermediate level of the quality policy trajectory, CQAHE produced annual reports on the quality reviews for 1993 to 1995. These reports were obtained prior to interviews so as not to waste interview time on material already available, and also to provide fodder for the interview questions. They were published by the Australian Government Publishing Service and were therefore readily available.

At the micro level of the quality policy trajectory, quality portfolios produced each year for the period 1993 to 1995 by each case-study university were examined for clues to the ways in which universities responded to the quality policy. Forster (1994) has described how 'company documentation' can reveal a great deal about the culture and image a company is trying to propagate, both internally to its own employees and externally to customers and competitors.

The original intention was to examine the three quality portfolios for 1993 to 1995 for all 36 public universities. A letter explaining the research and requesting a copy of portfolios was sent to the registrar of each university. There was, however, considerable sensitivity by a few institutions about their portfolios being in the public arena. In an increasingly competitive environment, disclosure of internal university details was becoming an issue, as further evidenced by subsequent concerns expressed by Vice-Chancellors about quality requirements infringing commercial confidentiality (Illing, 1997). Ultimately, and subsequent to several reminder prompts, there was a 100 per cent success rate in obtaining all quality portfolios from all universities for each of the three years 1993–1995.

However, despite the success in obtaining the documentation, a framework for analysing the portfolios to facilitate direct comparisons and contrasts across universities proved to be elusive. The variations both between universities and within any one university over the three years were enormous, rendering systematic examination problematic. Thus, I had some taste of the

diversity of approaches and subsequent difficulties in comparative analysis reported to me by the CQAHE respondents.

Newspapers, especially the Higher Education Supplement of
The Australian and the *Campus Review*, were useful data sources
in revealing the dynamics of the policy process at all levels of the
quality policy trajectory. In general these media furnished a
much more critical perspective than policy documents produced
by the policy making elite (Gewirtz and Ozga, 1994), especially
as they provided a conduit for voices of resistance from the
lower levels of the policy trajectory. However, as with other documents, care must be taken with newspaper articles as they also
actively construct a particular version of reality (May, 1993).
Newspapers did provide another valuable source for triangulation to 'locate' similarities and differences in perspective, both
within and between groups at different levels of the policy trajectory.

Interview data

Interviews were conducted at three levels of the quality policy
trajectory, and were a major component of the unique contribution of the study. Therefore, some time is spent here outlining
the approaches to interview data.

Access to suitable samples of respondents

Key informants were selected for interviews by non-probability
sampling techniques, also known as purposeful or purposive
sampling (May, 1993; Hornby and Symon, 1994; Miles and
Huberman, 1994) on the basis that the study called for 'specific
information from specific informants who are knowledgeable
about the process under consideration' (Hornby and Symon,
1994, p. 169). Whilst non-probability sampling can raise questions about 'skewed' samples (as opposed to random samples)
by clearly specifying the characteristics of the groups sampled,
this study used the approach by Goetz and LeCompte (1984) in
which generalisability is sought through comparability and
translatability.

Once the ideal respondents had been selected for the study,
the problem was to obtain their consent for an interview.
Walford (1994a) has made the point that access to key people

involved in promoting or implementing a particular initiative may be limited unless the researcher is identified as being 'on their side'. Elsewhere he emphasised that personal sponsorship can play an important part in gaining access, especially to powerful respondents (Walford, 1994b). Power is a relative concept, and in this study all of the respondents were more powerful than me as the researcher. Given my status as a student, personal sponsorship as a means of gaining access at all levels was invaluable. In the initial letter requesting an interview my two supervisors were named, and in most cases one or the other supervisor (sometimes both) was known to the potential respondent. For interview requests to CQAHE members, one supervisor who had worked with that committee wrote a separate letter introducing me. From the point of view of the respondent, not only could my supervisors vouch for my *bona fide* status but they would also be monitoring the ongoing products of my research. Of course it would have been a disadvantage if either of my supervisors had had an antagonistic relationship with any potential respondents. However, this did not appear to be the case.

Gewirtz and Ozga (1994, p. 193) reported that their access to a group of male policy-making elites was considerably eased because they were viewed by respondents as 'perfectly harmless'. They were both women, and in junior positions in their university, and were therefore not considered 'important'. Both of these factors perceived as access-easing by Gewirtz and Ozga (female gender and low status position) were relevant to me as the researcher in this project and, like them, I believe that some advantages ensued.

At the intermediate level of the policy trajectory, seven of the ten-member CQAHE committee were interviewed during 1995. The main criterion for selection of CQAHE respondents became a matter of geography, as I was based in Perth (on the west coast) and research funding covered a trip to Sydney (on the east coast), which would take in a majority of CQAHE members. CQAHE members elsewhere would have been contacted if there had not been a relatively consistent picture emerging from these seven informants. The CQAHE respondents sampled represented the main constituent groups – both 'old' and 'new' universities; the Department of Employment, Education and Training; and industry groups – so a cross-section of the different backgrounds and experiences that the members brought to CQAHE was included. Given the small size of the group and the importance of identifying respondent background in understanding their viewpoints, respondents were guaranteed that permission would be sought before quoting them directly (even anonymously), and all were happy with this arrangement.

At the micro level of the policy trajectory, six case-study universities (three each in the states of Western Australia and New South Wales) were chosen to examine the operation of the quality policy at localised sites. These institutions were selected as matched pairs of case studies labelled as 'traditional', 'alternative' and 'former college' types of universities, based on their historical contexts. Both case studies and multiple-site case studies are increasingly seen as attractive methodological tools (Tritter, 1995). According to Hartley (1994, p. 208), case studies 'shed light on the fine-grain detail of social processes in their appropriate context'. The issue of generalisability from case studies is a central one, but, according to Miles and Huberman (1994), the advantages of the *multi*-case analysis like that used here are to enhance generalisability and to deepen understanding and explanation. However, they also acknowledged that there are always tensions between the uniqueness of a particular case and the need for a more universal understanding of generic processes across different cases. They maintained that any particular case or site has 'a few properties it shares with *many* others, some properties it shares with *some* others, and some properties it shares with *no* others' (Miles and Huberman, 1994, p. 29).

At each of the six case-study universities, four institutional managers involved in constructing their university's quality submissions (portfolios and visits) were interviewed in 1995 (concurrent with the CQAHE interviews). At each case-study site contact was made with one senior manager, who in turn identified the key senior personnel involved in the quality process at that institution. As a check, during interviews all institutional manager respondents were asked to identify the main players in the quality policy process at their university and the same names kept coming up. Although the precise titles of respondent positions varied between universities, they were all chosen by a contact *in situ* on the basis of closest possible involvement in the preparation of quality submissions. Only one invitation to participate was declined, and that person nominated another manager as his substitute. Using this snowball sampling method (May, 1993; Hornby and Symon, 1994) access to the group was enhanced, as the senior manager who was first approached had in effect given approval to the research. However, the drawback that some respondents might then have felt obliged to reflect the particular perspective of the initial contact must also be recognised. This situation was most evident in one interview situation, when a respondent hesitated to answer several questions until he had conferred with the senior manager who had nominated him as his substitute for the interview. However, there were no other instances of nominating proxies, and on the whole I had the strong impression that individual respondents were reporting their own perceptions, even to the extent of identifying where their opinion was different from that of other members of the management group at their university. One institutional manager requested to see a transcript of the interview and subsequently removed reference to one name. All gave permission to be quoted anonymously.

At the mini-micro level of the policy trajectory, twelve grassroots academics were chosen at each case-study university for follow-up interviews during 1997. The twelve respondents from each site were made up of four from each of three different discipline areas (sciences, social sciences and education). There was only one refusal to participate, and a replacement was found without difficulty. No-one expressed a desire to see a transcript of the interview, and all agreed to be quoted, without sighting the selected quote, if their anonymity was maintained.

The structure and content of interviews

At all levels of the policy trajectory where interviews were used, the type of interview chosen fitted the general category of 'semi-structured' (May, 1993), 'structured open-response' (King, 1994) or 'general interview' guide (Patton, 1990). Whichever label is used, the approach was somewhere in the middle of a continuum between highly structured/standardised schedules and the antithesis of unstructured conversations. On the one hand it was important to maintain control of the interview to ensure that all questions were asked of all respondents to enable comparisons and contrasts both within and between different levels of the trajectory; on the other hand it was important to have the flexibility to use probes to elicit more detailed responses and also to alter the sequence or combination of questions if the need arose. In Kogan's words, the aim was to 'keep a balance between structured and controlled enquiry and dynamic interaction with the matter being researched' (Kogan, 1994, p. 79).

Interview questions at the intermediate (CQAHE) and micro (institutional manager) levels were organised to reflect the structure of the quality model that emerged from the macro (minister and Higher Education Council) level of policy text production. That is, the main components to the interview schedule focussed on *inputs* or the context leading to the initiation of the quality policy; *processes* undertaken to operationalise the policy; and *outcomes* or effects of the policy. The same questions were asked of CQAHE and institutional managers about their perceptions of the context, and about their perceptions of the effects of the policy across the higher education sector. Questions about the processes involved were inevitably different for CQAHE and institutional manager respondents at these different levels of the policy trajectory. Figure 5.1 illustrates the structure of the interview for CQAHE and institutional manager respondents.

The original intention was to mirror this meta-structure of inputs–processes–outcomes for the interview schedule with grassroots academics (mini-micro level) as well. However, trialling revealed that this would not be possible because grassroots academics could not make connections between the quality

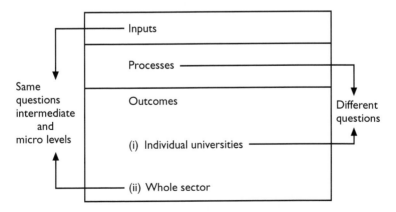

Figure 5.1 Structure of the interviews at intermediate and micro levels

policy and their daily working lives. By contrast, they had a great deal to say about the effects of the increasing number of policies to enhance accountability of universities and academics to government (Vidovich and Currie, 1998), and thus the interview theme was broadened to the wider issue of accountability.

In terms of the content of individual interview questions, Patton (1990, pp. 290–291) distinguished six question types: experience/behaviour; opinion/values; feeling; knowledge; sensory; and background/demographic. The principal foci in this study were 'experience/behaviour' questions, which are aimed at 'eliciting descriptions of experiences, behaviours, actions, and activities that would have been observable had the observer been present', and also 'opinion/values' questions which 'tell us what people *think* about some issue'. Although there were some knowledge questions, this domain (which deals with factual information) was covered more by using documents, so that interviews could focus on a deeper understanding of the issues. Across the three sets of interviews, all of Patton's categories of question content were included.

Interviews with CQAHE members (intermediate level) were longer and less structured than interviews at the institutional (micro and mini-micro) level, as CQAHE respondents had more insider knowledge of the quality policy process to be explored. Interview schedules for CQAHE members were often individually constructed to draw on the different interests and expertise each brought to CQAHE. Questions were tailored around knowing the backgrounds of each respondent, which were obtained from earlier CQAHE reports and from one of my supervisors who had worked with these people as a member of CQAHE teams visiting universities.

Each of the three sets of interview questions at the three levels (intermediate, micro and mini-micro level) were trialled with a relevant participant who was also a 'critical friend'. I felt more comfortable starting the interviews with someone I knew, and I asked each critical friend to provide feedback on how easy/difficult, relevant/peripheral they found the questions. Changes were minor for CQAHE and institutional management levels but, as indicated previously, the whole nature of the questions changed for the grassroots academics. Thus, trialling enabled appropriate modifications to both the structure and the content of the interviews.

Establishing rapport

Rapport between researcher and respondent is essential if respondents are to be encouraged to reflect critically on their experiences. May (1993) defined rapport in terms of building a sense of trust and cooperation that facilitates a free flow of information. Patton (1990) included another dimension by tying rapport to neutrality in the relationship between the respondent and the interviewer. The following excerpt from Patton (1990, pp. 316–317) reflects the approach taken in this study:

> Rapport must be established in such a way that it does not undermine neutrality concerning what the person tells me. Neutrality means that the person being interviewed can tell me anything without engendering either my favour or disfavour with regard to the content of the response ... At the same time I am neutral with regard to the content of what is being said to me, I care very much that that person is willing to share with me what they are saying ... I want to convey to them that their knowledge, experiences, attitudes, and feelings are important. Yet, I will not judge them for the content of what they say to me.

Similarly, Kogan (1994, p. 73) maintained that 'the researcher has to behave so as to make the interviewee feel an important contributor to a worthwhile exercise'. Despite the obvious benefits of building rapport, Walford (1994b) cautioned that care must be taken not to be so concerned with rapport that less comfortable issues are avoided. He reported the strategy used by some interviewers of challenging the respondent face-on if his or her answers are evasive. I tried this on one occasion (with both a smile and heart palpitations) to achieve some degree of success in obtaining a more detailed and reflective response, but the social distance between researcher and respondent might well be a mitigating factor in this strategy.

At the outset of each interview, establishing rapport/trust with the respondent was a priority. I wanted to present as a highly motivated and well-organised researcher who had done her homework (Walford, 1994b), and therefore would not waste the respondent's time. However, I also wanted to present a friendly, open manner to invite interchange. Trust was furthered by requesting permission to tape (not assuming), offering that the respondent was welcome to read the transcript before any analysis and reporting, and assuring anonymity for quotation. Only one respondent took up the offer to read the transcript, and apart from deleting reference to one name he left the transcript intact.

Perhaps a pointer to the high degree of rapport with many respondents across the three levels of the trajectory was the large number of offers to extend the interview beyond the 45 minutes to an hour that had been requested and agreed. Many respondents, especially at the CQAHE and institutional levels, said that they were finding the interviews a good opportunity to reflect and bring together their own thoughts on the topical, and rapidly changing, notions of quality and accountability in higher education. There were also numerous offers to continue informal discussion on the topic over coffee or lunch after the interview.

In particular, CQAHE respondents were highly cooperative and gave generously of their time, with interviews ranging from one hour to two and a half hours (three interviews lasted longer than two hours). This exceptionally high level of cooperation raises the question of the extent to which respondents were using their powerful status to present their own roles in the policy process in the best possible light, and also to smooth over any problems and controversies. Gewirtz and Ozga (1994) referred to this phenomenon as the 'rose-tinted spectacles syndrome'. Fitz and Halpin (1994b) cautioned against uncritical acceptance of elite narratives of the policy process as this would result in the researcher simply reproducing the discourse of the powerful, or as Batteson and Ball (1995, p. 202) put it, '"going native" and being persuaded to see it as "they" do'. Whilst acknowledging that the CQAHE respondents were in an ideal position to control the interview to get their own message across, with the use of probes and occasional challenges I worked at counteracting this effect.

Taping the interviews

Permission was granted by all respondents, except one, to tape the interview. Brief notes of key phrases were also taken during the interview as an insurance against tape failure, which was the case with one respondent. In that instance, the routine check of the tape after leaving the respondent's office revealed that it was inaudible (the distance between the tape recorder and respondent was too great for the volume of the respondent's voice). I immediately typed up the interview while my memory was fresh, and the interview notes provided invaluable mental triggers. I changed to a more powerful recording device after that interview.

For the one respondent who did not want to be taped, I took copious notes and can verify Patton's (1990, p. 348) point that 'the interactive nature of in-depth interviewing can be seriously affected by the attempt to take verbatim notes during the interview'. Some researchers (Kogan, 1994) make the point that recorders can inhibit dialogue, but I believe that my respondents from largely academic backgrounds were comfortable with the recording, especially as many had used recording devices in their own research. However, I agree with Thompson (1996) that whilst the audio-tape recorder is 'an empowering and enabling research instrument', its potential to mediate both the experience of the researcher and the nature of the research should not be discounted.

Analysing the interview data

Miles and Huberman (1994) have described qualitative analysis as three concurrent flows of activity: data reduction, data display and conclusion drawing/verification. A central element of data reduction is the coding process defined by them as 'attaching meaningful labels to data chunks' (p. 89). Similarly, King (1994) outlined the use of a template approach where text is analysed using a codebook that will be modified as exposure to the data increases, and Hartley (1994) emphasised the revision of categories as the processes of data interrogation and theory building continue. Strauss and Corbin (1990) have described a grounded theory approach to developing categories by asking questions about the data and making comparisons to identify similarities and differences. Categories are developed according to their properties (characteristics) and dimensions (location of a property along a continuum, such as high to low or more to less).

In this study, preliminary codes developed as logical extensions from the interview questions were modified extensively as data emerged during the ongoing analysis. In general terms, Miles and Huberman's sequence for abstracting key themes from the data was adopted, beginning with first-level coding, then proceeding to second-level or pattern coding and then to memoing for deriving more general themes. By including extensive respondent quotes in the reporting of data, the reader is able to judge the effectiveness with which the artificially contrived categories represent the raw data. That is, the reader is able to move closer to the first-hand experiences of the respondents rather than always relying on the researcher's second-hand interpretation of the data, thereby making their own assessments of validity.

The NUD.IST (Non-numerical Unstructured Data Indexing Searching and Theorising) software program was used to analyse the larger number of interviews at the mini-micro level in this study. Miles and Huberman (1994) have identified the particular strengths of NUD.IST in coding (attaching key words to segments of text), search and retrieval (locating relevant segments of text), memoing (writing reflective commentaries for deeper analysis) and theory building (developing conceptually coherent explanations).

Holbrook and Butcher (1996) provided an overview of the polarised opinion associated with the use of computer software for qualitative research. The positives usually emphasise the improved validity (interpretative and theoretical as well as generalisability) derived from the greater visibility of the research process because there is an audit trail for others to follow and critique. The arguments against using computer software include distancing the researcher from the data, overfragmentation of the data, and the strait-jacket effect of needing to generate 'neat' data to plug into the computer. In this study, I chose to 'sit on the fence' by using computer software for only one of the three sets of interview data. Coding by hand was used for the smaller numbers of earlier respondent interviews at the CQAHE (intermediate) and institutional manager (micro) levels of the trajectory. NUD.IST was employed for analysing interviews of grassroots academics (mini-micro level) who were asked a different set of questions at a later point in the trajectory. However, as with coding by hand, the NUD.IST tree of index nodes or categories evolved as data analysis progressed.

Conclusion

Education policy sociology is increasingly characterised by theoretical and methodological eclecticism (Troyna, 1994; Ball, 1997; Taylor, 1997). This study was designed to draw strength from a certain degree of eclecticism by bringing together different theories and methods to illuminate the policy processes associated with the ascendancy of accountability in general, and quality in particular, in Australian higher education of the 1990s.

At all stages, the methods were closely interwoven with the theoretical framework. A quality policy trajectory was constructed to move through the contexts of influence, policy text production and practice. Policy actor groups at four different levels were identified, and then the data which were collected from documents and interviews at these four levels were analysed. Triangulation both within and between levels was designed to increase the reliability and validity, or dependability, credibility and transferability (Miles and Huberman, 1994), of the research findings. With movement through different levels of the trajectory, the number of interview respondents increased between the intermediate level, the micro level, and the mini-micro level. This hierarchy of sample sizes reflects the different sizes of the total populations at each level. Thus, one might visualise the extraction of a wedge of samples to reveal some of the lived experiences of the quality policy process.

A number of books and articles within the field of education policy sociology (Fitz and Halpin, 1994b; Walford, 1994b) encourage the practice of 'researching up' or 'studying up', referring to the investigation of the role of 'the powerful' in education policy making. This study accepted the challenge by moving through a hierarchy of respondents who were all more powerful than the researcher. 'Researching up' has both advantages and disadvantages from a methodological perspective. On the one hand Gewirtz and Ozga (1994) believe that access to the policy elite can be enhanced if the researcher is deemed to be 'perfectly harmless', but on the other hand this elite is in a strong position to take control of the interview, with the effect of simply reproducing the discourse of the powerful (Fitz and Halpin, 1994b). In the end I was satisfied that everyone's interests were being served by researching this high profile, new policy direction in Australian higher education.

To conclude, I would like to make a final comment on the substantive topic of the study – 'quality' policy as a mechanism for
increasing accountability, and also for promulgating changes in
the nature of accountability in higher education from professional and democratic forms to managerial and market forms.
Universities have traditionally occupied a distinctive social position in terms of both enrichment and a critical voice in society.
However, the growing privileging of economic constructions of
accountability, and the growing instrumental emphasis forged
by governments adopting market ideologies, threaten the unique
contributions that universities make. I would argue that the
balance between accountability and autonomy (for both universities and academics) needs to be continually renegotiated in the
long-term interests of society. For more detailed discussions of
the findings of this study, see Vidovich and Porter (1997, 1999),
and Vidovich (2001). For subsequent analysis of continually
evolving quality policy in Australian higher education into the
twenty first century, see Vidovich (2002).

Bibliography

Baldwin, P. (1991) *Higher Education: Quality and Diversity in the 1990s.*
Canberra: Australian Government Publishing Service.

Ball, S. J. (1990) *Politics and Policy Making in Education.* London: Routledge.

Ball, S. J. (1994a) Researching inside the state: issues in the interpreta-
tion of elite interviews. *In:* D. Halpin and B. Troyna (eds), *Researching
Education Policy: Ethical and Methodological Issues,* pp. 107–120.
London: Falmer Press.

Ball, S. J. (1994b) *Education Reform: A Critical and Post-structural Approach.*
Buckingham and Philadelphia: Open University Press.

Ball, S. J. (1997) Policy sociology and critical social research: a personal
review of recent education policy and policy research. *British Educational Research Journal* 23(3): 257–274.

Batteson, C. and Ball, S. J. (1995) Autobiographies and interviews as
means of 'access' to elite policy making in education. *British Journal of
Educational Studies* 43(2): 201–216.

Bessant, B. (1995) Corporate management and its penetration of the university administration and government. *Australian Universities' Review*
38(1): 59–62.

Bowe, R., Ball, S. J. and Gold, A. (1992) *Reforming Education and Changing
Schools.* London: Routledge.

Cassell, C. and Symon, G. (1994) Qualitative research in work contexts. *In*: C. Cassell and G. Symon (eds), *Qualitative Methods in Organizational Research*, pp. 1–13. London: Sage.

Codd, J. (1988) The construction and deconstruction of educational policy documents. *Journal of Education Policy* 3(3): 235–248.

Dale, R. (1989) *The State and Education Policy*. Milton Keynes: Open University Press.

Fitz, J. and Halpin, D. (1994a) Implementation research and education policy: practice and prospects. *British Journal of Educational Studies* 42(1): 53–69.

Fitz, J. and Halpin, D. (1994b) Ministers and mandarins: educational research in elite settings. *In*: G. Walford (ed.), *Researching the Powerful in Education*, pp. 32–50. London: University College London Press.

Forster, N. (1994) The analysis of company documentation. *In*: C. Cassell and G. Symon (eds), *Qualitative Methods in Organizational Research*, pp. 147–166. London: Sage.

Gale, T. (1994) Beyond caricature: exploring theories of educational policy production and implementation. *The Australian Educational Researcher* 21(2): 1–12.

Gewirtz, S. and Ozga, J. (1994) Interviewing the education policy elite. *In*: G. Walford (ed.), *Researching the Powerful in Education*, pp. 186–203, London: University College London Press.

Gilbert, R. and Low, P. (1994) Discourse and power in education: analysing institutional processes in schools. *Australian Educational Researcher* 21(3): 1–24.

Gillborn, D. (1994) The micro-politics of macro reform. *British Journal of Sociology of Education* 15(2): 147–164.

Goetz, J. P. and LeCompte, M. D. (1984) Characteristics and origins of educational ethnography. *In*: J. P. Goetz and M. D. LeCompte (eds), *Ethnography and Qualitative Design in Educational Research*, pp. 1–32. London: Academic Press.

Hajer, M. A. (1995) *The Politics of Environmental Discourse*. Oxford: Clarendon Press.

Hartley, J. F. (1994) Case studies in organisational research. *In*: C. Cassell and G. Symon (eds), *Qualitative Methods in Organizational Research*, pp. 208–229. London: Sage.

Holbrook, A. and Butcher, L. (1996) Uses of qualitative data analysis software in educational research: the literature, the hard questions and some specific research applications. *The Australian Educational Researcher* 23(3): 55–80.

Hornby, P. and Symon, G. (1994) Tracer studies. *In*: C. Cassell and G. Symon (eds), *Qualitative Methods in Organizational Research*, pp. 167–186. London: Sage.

Illing, D. (1997) Quality reviews 'blow secrets'. *The Australian Higher Education Supplement*, 26 Mar, 33.

Illing, D. (1998) New era heightens clash of uni factions, *The Australian Higher Education Supplement*, 11 Feb, 35.

Jordan, S. and Yeomans, D. (1995) Critical ethnography: problems in contemporary theory and practice, *British Journal of Sociology of Education* 16(3): 389–408.

Kamler, B., Comber, B. and Cook, J. (1997) Introduction: critical discourse analysis, or life after the linguistic turn. *Discourse: Studies in the Cultural Politics of Education* 18(3): 325–327.

King, N. (1994) The qualitative research interview. *In*: C. Cassell and G. Symon (eds), *Qualitative Methods in Organizational Research*, pp. 14–36. London: Sage.

Kogan, M. (1994) Researching the powerful in education and elsewhere. *In*: G. Walford (ed.), *Researching the Powerful in Education*, pp. 67–80. London: University College London Press.

LeCompte, M. D. and Preissle, J. (1993) *Ethnography and Qualitative Design in Educational Research*. San Diego, CA: Academic Press Inc.

Lingard, B. (1993) The changing state of policy production in education: some Australian reflections on the state of policy sociology. *International Studies in Sociology of Education* 3(1): 25–47.

Lingard, B. (1996) Review essay: educational policy making in a postmodern state. On Stephen J. Ball's education reform: a critical and post-structural approach. *Australian Educational Researcher* 23(1): 65–91.

Marshall, H. (1994) Discourse analysis in an occupational context. *In*: C. Cassell and G. Symon (eds), *Qualitative Methods in Organizational Research*, pp. 91–106. London: Sage.

May, T. (1993) *Social Research: Issues, Methods and Process*. Buckingham: Open University Press.

Miles, M. B. and Huberman, A. M. (1994) *Qualitative Data Analysis: An Expanded Sourcebook*. Thousand Oaks, CA: Sage.

Ozga, J. (1987) Studying education policy through the lives of policy makers: an attempt to close the macro-micro gap. *In*: S. Walker and L. Barton (eds), *Changing Policies, Changing Teachers: New Directions for Schooling?*, pp. 138–150. Milton Keynes: Open University Press.

Ozga, J. (1990) Policy research and policy theory: a comment on Fitz and Halpin. *Journal of Education Policy* 5(4): 359–362.

Ozga, J. and Gewirtz, S. (1994) Sex, lies and audiotape: Interviewing the education policy elite. *In*: D. Halpin and B. Troyna (eds), *Researching Education Policy: Ethical and Methodological Issues*, pp. 121–135. London: Falmer Press.

Patton, M. Q. (1990) *Qualitative Evaluation and Research Methods*. Newbury Park, CA: Sage.

Prunty, J. J. (1985) Signpost for a critical educational policy analysis. *Australian Journal of Education* 29(2): 133–140.

Raab, C. D. (1994a) Where are we now? reflections on the sociology of education policy. In: D. Halpin and B. Troyna (eds), *Researching Education Policy: Ethical and Methodological Issues*, pp. 16–30. London: Falmer Press.

Raab, C. D. (1994b) Theorising the governance of education. *British Journal of Educational Studies* 42(1): 6–21.

Skillington, T. (1997) Politics and the struggle to define: a discourse analysis of the framing strategies of competing actors in a 'new' participatory forum. *British Journal of Sociology*, 48(3): 493–513.

Strauss, A. and Corbin, J. (1990) Coding procedures. In: A. Strauss and J. Corbin (eds), *Basics of Qualitative Research*, pp. 56–115. London: Sage.

Taylor, S. (1997) Critical policy analysis: exploring contexts, texts and consequences. *Discourse: Studies in the Cultural Politics of Education* 18(1): 23–35.

Thompson, D. J. (1996) The tape-recorder as a mediating factor in research. *The Australian Educational Researcher* 23(3): 1–12.

Tritter, J. (1995) The context of educational policy research: changed constraints, new methodologies and ethical complexities. *British Journal of Sociology of Education* 16(3): 419–430.

Troyna, B. (1994) Reforms, research and being reflexive about being reflective. In: D. Halpin and B. Troyna (eds), *Researching Education Policy: Ethical and Methodological Issues*, pp. 1–14. London: Falmer Press.

Vanstone, A. (1996) *Higher Education Budget Statement*. Canberra: Australian Government Publishing Service.

Vidovich, L. (1998) 'Quality' as accountability in Australian higher education of the 1990s: a policy trajectory. Unpublished PhD Thesis, Murdoch University, Australia.

Vidovich, L. (2001) That chameleon 'quality': the multiple and contradictory discourses of 'quality' policy in Australian higher education. *Discourse: Studies in the Cultural Politics of Education* 2(2): 249–261.

Vidovich, L. (2002) Quality assurance in Australian higher education: globalisation and 'steering at a distance'. *Higher Education* 43: 391–408.

Vidovich, L. and Currie, J. (1998) Changing accountability and autonomy at the 'chalkface' of academic work in Australia. In: J. Currie and J. Newson (eds), *Globalization and Universities: Critical Perspectives*. Thousand Oaks, CA: Sage.

Vidovich, L. and Porter, P. (1997) The recontextualization of 'quality' in Australian higher education. *The Journal of Education Policy* 12(4): 233–252.

Vidovich, L. and Porter, P. (1999) 'Quality' policy in Australian higher education of the 1990s: university perspectives. *The Journal of Education Policy* 14(6): 567–586.

Walford, G. (1994a) A new focus on the powerful. *In*: G. Walford (ed.), *Researching the Powerful in Education*, pp. 2–11. London: University College London Press.

Walford, G. (1994b) Reflections on researching the powerful. *In*: G. Walford (ed.), *Researching the Powerful in Education*, pp. 222–231. London: University College London Press.

Chapter 6

Reflections on a qualitative investigation of critical literacies and the teaching of English

Peter Stewart and Marnie O'Neill

Introduction

This chapter reflects on a study premised on a notion that research into the meanings of individual teachers involved in critical literacy (CL) programmes is important, since it can help to clarify whether they are perceiving, adapting and facilitating CL in ways consistent with its radical aims. There is no common definition of CL. Nevertheless, the literature agrees that it refers to a project concerned with inculcating in students a critical awareness of socio-cultural issues as represented by texts; students are to be literate in methods of analysing the way social power operates in texts. However, most of the literature attempting to define CL ignores what these definitions might mean for and to individual English teachers. Few texts are concerned that competing definitions may confuse or alienate teachers.

Data on teachers' perspectives on CL were collected through semi-structured interviews with four participants. All were English teachers at an Australian high school, divided equally by gender and aged between 25 and 45 years. The interviews provided emergent data that were followed-up in subsequent interviews or informal conversations. A CL professional development course in which the teachers participated was also observed, during which notes were taken. As CL is a set of differing (often competing) discourses, an adaptation of discourse analysis was used to analyse all the data. The theoretical perspective of symbolic interactionism enabled the researcher to take into account the individual agency and responsibility of the participants; factors that discourse analysis tends to disregard.

This study found that teachers were negotiating CL as a

broadly-based English ethical discourse, confusing radical English with earlier models of facilitating an affective change in students. This confusion was attributed to:

- The confusions of CL theory, with its liberal-humanist survivals, its neo-Marxist idealism and its poststructuralist relativism/pessimism
- The constitution of English teachers as teachers, informed by the three competing discourses that are basic to subject English: rhetoric, aesthetics and ethics
- Owing to a weakness in theory, the current dominance of this non-specific ethical discourse in English education. An outcome of the confusion among English teachers is the highly conflictive nature of English pedagogy and teaching.

The research questions

The narrow teaching roles offered by the CL literature, the lack of general agreement on a CL definition, and the assumption that teachers will respond to the politics of CL in a monolithic way influenced the development of the five necessarily broad questions that directed and influenced data collection in this study. These questions were:

1   What does CL mean to some individual English teachers?
2   What is the relationship between the political agendas of CL and the beliefs and values of these individual teachers?
3   What student outcomes (in the broadest sense) do English teachers believe they are facilitating when inculcating CL?
4   What ambivalences – if any – do English teachers have concerning their relationships with CL?
5   What are some of the implications for teachers and CL theory in the meanings English teachers attribute to CL?

The main elements of the theoretical perspective of this study, symbolic interactionism, are outlined, followed by the research methodology that was employed, discourse analysis. The relationship between the theoretical perspective and the analytical technique is discussed. Following this, details of the processes of sample selection, data collection and analysis are provided.

Theoretical perspective: symbolic interactionism

The main assumptions underpinning this study approximated the three principles embodied in the interpretive approach known as symbolic interactionism (SI). SI derives from the hermeneutic/interpretative paradigm in social and educational research. It was formulated in the Chicago School of Social Interactionism by George Mead, Herbert Blumer and others. Blumer's three principles of SI are:

1   Individuals attribute personal meanings to phenomena and act towards them in a social environment on the basis of these personal meanings
2   Meaning develops from the way other people act towards the person in relation to the phenomenon
3   Meaning is negotiated, maintained and adopted in a process of interpretation.

SI assumes that meaning is never a fixed entity. Meaning is always undergoing a process of adjustment or change through the input of fresh information derived from a social context. However, it is individuals who develop their social roles in relation to others; the 'self is always in process' (Osborne and Van Loon, 1996, p. 79). This study followed this assumption, which is contingent on the belief that the individual and his or her social interaction must be taken into account – i.e. that the individual and society 'are inseparable units'. Two strengths of SI as identified by Hargreaves were of particular relevance to this study. First, it has an 'appreciative capacity' [which allows for exploration of] social interaction from the point of view of the actor' (Woods, 1992, p. 392). Second, it has a 'designatory capacity [allowing articulation of ostensibly] taken-for-granted or common sense knowledge [which provides a] language for discourse about [the area of study]'.

Discourse analysis

Discourse analysis (DA) is a research methodology with no 'overarching unifying theory common to all types [of academic disciplines]' (Punch, 1998, p. 305). The study used an adaptation of the type of DA that was derived from European social philosophy and cultural analysis, which attempts to show how institutions, practices and individuals operate through discourses, with talk and texts operating as social practices. Discourses are socially constructed and recognised ways of doing and being in the world, which integrate and regulate ways of acting, thinking, feeling, using language, and believing (Lankshear, 1997a, p. 402). Punch (1998, p. 305) paraphrases Worrall's definition of the term 'discourse': it refers to 'all aspects of communication ... not only content, but its author (who says it?), its authority (on what grounds?), its audience (to whom [and] its objective ... (in order to achieve what?)'.

DA attempts to negotiate 'new phenomena, [which entails] critical analyses of text-based, postmodern cultures and economies' (Luke, 1997, p. 56), the assumption being that:

> ... identities and affiliated phenomena such as 'class', 'race' and 'gender' cannot be viewed as having prior essential characteristics independent of their formation and representation in [cultural] discourse.

DA assumes that there is a connection between the social construction of essential characteristics such as stereotypes, and dominant power structures, which perpetuate 'regimes of representation' (Macedo, 1994, p. 36) in their own interest – i.e. it emphasises 'the interrelationship between accounts [for example, what is said] and [social] hierarchies' (Punch, 1998, p. 309). DA attempts to dismantle constructed accounts, so that the political elements of their construction may be identified.

DA is problematic in that it promotes a tendency to assign political labels (reactionary, progressive etc.) to elements of texts or 'accounts', with little scrutiny of the history of the use of these labels, or their applicability to the complex origins and motivations that produce types of language usage (Steele, 1997). It is often assumed by cultural critics that language exists in a vacuum of political reproduction (Paglia, 1992). The assumption here is that there is always an individual person behind every text and account whose experiences and values might usually be determined culturally, but the extent and 'nature' of this determinism are questions that are too ambiguous and complex to answer with certainty.

Although the emphasis in DA's dismantling of 'constructed accounts' (Punch, 1998, p. 309) is often to reveal connections between 'power and ideology', the adaptation of DA used in the study to which this chapter relates is more concerned with a wider paradigm; the space where this 'heterogeneous discipline ... finds its unity ... an interest in the context and cultural influences which affect language in use'. This adaptation does not preclude the notion that hierarchies operate and are maintained through language. However, it takes what might be considered a middle-ground position by assuming that the wider context of language usage (and culture itself) may not necessarily be explicable through the strictly progressivist or radical discourses of cultural studies. The liberal position of the study allowed cultural studies (and CL) to be read as problematic discourses operating in the field of Australian education, as opposed to techniques of analysis conducive to a form of (obscure) politico-transcendental salvation (Lankshear and Lawler, 1987; Gee, 1997).

Theorists have pointed out that it is 'difficult to describe and codify explicit procedures that are used in discourse analysis' (Punch, 1998, p. 308). However, five conditions, adaptations of which which were the basis for the way DA methodology was undertaken in the study, recur. They are:

1   Variation used as a lever – the fact of difference as it exists in the accounts of research participants is a pre-condition that allows for the comparison and contrast of language used by the sample group. This enables the researcher to test a discourse's viability as it emerges, i.e. to take into account both the contradictions in individual accounts and group accounts and assess how representative the emerging discourse is of the individual or of the group.

2   Reading the detail – in DA, as with most analyses derived from cultural studies, the data are read closely so that contradictions and inconsistencies may be identified.

3   Looking for rhetorical organisation – given the assumption that the accounts often derive from cultural contexts, the use of rhetorical language is identified. This language operates as rhetoric in that it tends to locate the speaker in the process of maintaining or defending a cultural discourse at the expense of others. Rhetorical usage represents less the

communication of considered opinion than reproduction of a cultural assumption.

4   Looking for accountability – establishing what the speaker has to lose or gain by using language in a particular way, contingent on the assumption that language operates to maintain culturally dominant hierarchies. It is a method of establishing whether the speaker is using language to normalise his or her position in the *status quo*.

5   Cross-referencing discourse studies – adaptation of various uses and outlines of DA, taking into account the wider field of cultural studies.

The relationship between symbolic interactionism and discourse analysis

The theoretical perspective of SI qualified the use of DA in the study. SI assumes that meaning is derived from the social interaction of individuals, while DA is concerned with the analysis of the results of this making of meaning, which are attributed to the maintenance of a social hierarchy. The allowance of SI for an 'appreciative capacity' (Woods, 1992, p. 392) enables the researcher to focus on this interaction from the point of view of the participants, i.e. in an empathetic sense. This is consistent with SI being at the 'individualistic end of social theory' (Osborne and Van Loon, 1996, p. 78), concerned with questions of individual agency. The 'designatory capacity' (Woods, 1992, p. 392) of SI assumes that that which will be provided by the participant is of use in itself. It assumes that the language used by the participant represents and provides a way of speaking about the wider context of, for example, the various discourses of both teachers and theorists that make up the CL discourse. The designatory capacity values the opinion of the participant, and assumes his or her colloquial language is as diagnostic of issues as academic language.

A main assumption of the study, as opposed to much DA (Lankshear *et al.*, 1997a), was that the participants were not merely representations of various discourses that exist to perpetuate dominant social hierarchies, but that their individual meanings operated in a process of continual adaptation and change. These are dependent on circumstance, experience, interaction, need – and a degree of personal agency that cultural criticism has difficulty in addressing (Steele, 1997). In SI, it is the self that is 'always in process' (Osborne and Van Loon, 1996, p. 79). The appreciative capacity of SI allowed the researcher to take into account – in an empathetic way – the flux of personal meaning, rather than mainly attribute that meaning to a set of fixed political notions somehow embedded in language.

This is not to argue (to reverse the popular cliché) that everything isn't politics, but that the form politics takes does not necessarily represent a location on the classic political spectrum, which many cultural critics seem to assume in their use of terms such as 'progressive' and 'reactionary' (Lankshear and Lawler, 1987; Macedo, 1994; Lankshear, 1997a). In this context, the empathetic, appreciative capacity allows for a degree of 'negative capability' (Rosenbaum, 1998, p. xi), as formulated by Keats, i.e. 'the ability to tolerate uncertainty without the "irritable reaching" for certainty'; a useful antidote to the political certainty (Hunter, 1994) that many cultural critics aspire to or operate from, which is rarely given the same scrutiny as capitalist 'productions of power' (Lankshear, 1997a, p. 407). However, it was the assumption of the study that the broader cultural contexts affect the use of language, and this language represents (and may be analysed as) discourse to a large extent.

Participant selection

The study was concerned with establishing the relationship individual English teachers have with the theory and practice of CL by investigating the meanings they ascribe to them. The participants in this study were all subject English teachers from a large state high school in an eastern suburb of Perth. The school had a reputation for social problems. Although research conducted in a single site is problematic in terms of its representativeness, it was decided to undertake research in one high school for three reasons:

1   There is little precedent for an investigation into the meanings individual teachers attribute to CL. It was considered prudent to choose a single site on the assumption that, given the qualitative, in-depth nature of the enterprise, this would supply enough data for an original area for research.
2   The chosen school was a potential source of rich data – not

only was a new CL policy being introduced to the English department in the year the research was undertaken, but the teachers also participated in a CL professional development course during the research. The English department was a site of debate, adaptation and change with regard to CL – i.e. the teachers were formulating a conscious relationship with CL during the course of the research and establishing ways that it might be best facilitated in their classrooms. This situation also provided an opportunity to investigate how the meanings teachers were attributing to CL were being influenced by their colleagues.

3   The fact that the school was a state institution with a reputation for being in a 'rough' area provided a context that was also relevant to the study. The teachers were sensitive to the wider social issues that concern much of CL theory (see, for example, Lankshear, 1987, 1997b; New London Group, 1996), with their emphasis on the need to critique the postmodern, socio-cultural representations of new capitalism that normalise and pathologise youth unemployment, despair, crime and poverty. In the preliminary conversations with the English department it was established that the teachers believed there to be a high incidence of these phenomena in the social environment in which the school exists. The implications these have for the vocational futures of the students in the 'new world order [of] work' (Lankshear, 1997b, p. 310) were recognised by the English department as influences on its attitude towards, and facilitation of, CL.

The research was initiated two months after the inception of the school's CL programme. By this time the teachers had acquired considerable practical experience in CL facilitation, and had accumulated much anecdotal evidence. The fact that the professional development course was not held until a month into the research enabled the researcher to interview teachers with practical experience of CL facilitation and a growing theoretical perspective.

Due to the necessity of gathering enough data from individual teachers to analyse, it was decided to extract a sample of participants from the English department. This sampling was undertaken by the researcher through initial informal discussions with teachers, and through the intermediary of the head of department – those who seemed most willing to talk of their relationship with CL and those who considered themselves to have enough to talk about were asked for interviews. This resulted in a sample of four teachers (A, B, C and D), divided equally by gender and who consisted of approximately 50 per cent of the members of the department. Except for one teacher, all the participants were less than 48 years old, the national average age of teachers. All had at least begun their education under the declining influence of the functionalist/traditionalist model and the rising influence of the personal growth model in the early 1970s. Therefore, any adaptations of CL they had made were potentially influenced by older conceptions of English, i.e. the teachers were representative of the average teacher who had experienced three subject English paradigm shifts during their life. This sample provided a large amount of data in the form of interview transcripts and enough variation for the purposes of comparison during data analysis.

Data collection

The use of SI as a theoretical perspective and DA as a research method made it necessary to apply a qualitative research strategy (Woods, 1992; Punch, 1998). This entailed conducting semi-structured, in-depth interviews with the four participants. The data was obtained through the following stages:

1   After establishing which teachers were prepared to discuss their relationship with CL, through informal discussion and the advice of the head of department, the researcher asked the four teachers to sign a consent form that informed them that they were under no obligation to give information, and that its incorporation in the study was subject to their veto.

2   Initial interviews of one to one-and-a-half hours each were conducted at times and locations convenient for the teachers. This usually meant during a teacher's 'class free' time in the school media room, although on one occasion an interview was conducted in a teacher's home. These initial semi-structured, in-depth interviews were the most comprehensive. All were taped, and notes were made so that major themes might be provisionally identified, elucidated and subjected to later analysis. The informal, flexible nature of

the interviews enabled the participant and researcher to discuss a variety of issues in a comfortable atmosphere, and provided opportunities to pursue issues that emerged in the course of the discussions in an unrestricted way. The language adopted by the researcher in these interviews was consistent with that used by the individual teacher – jargon and technical terms with which the teachers seemed uncomfortable (or admitted to being unfamiliar) were avoided by the researcher in favour of the teachers' own vocabulary as it presented itself in the interview. This was done in the context of SI's 'designatory capacity' (Woods, 1992), which assumes that the language used by the participants, although often unorthodox by theoretical standards, has value in itself and corresponds to the subject under discussion, regardless of how abstract its provenance. This allowed the participants the comfort of expressing themselves in their own words throughout the interview, and provided examples of the teachers' 'natural' use of language for use during analysis. Although the interviews were conducted in ways that allowed the participants to be as comfortable and 'in control' as possible, and elaboration and initiative were encouraged, they were closely guided by the research questions and the aim of the study – establishing the meanings individual teachers attribute to CL in theory and practice. Before the interviews were initiated their purpose was made clear to the teachers, and all questions asked by the researcher were framed in a way that made their relevance to the research as clear as possible.

3   The teachers were observed participating in a CL professional development course. Due to difficulties the department had with obtaining an appointment with the facilitator that was amenable to the school's timetable, the professional development course was conducted later in the research than was expected. However, by the time the course was held at the school the teachers had gained enough experience with facilitating CL to engage in discussion and debate with the facilitator. This enabled observation of how the teachers reconciled their experience with the academic/theoretical conception of CL. The researcher participated in the course by taking part in small group discussions and exercises with the teachers; however, this

participation was minimal. The researcher's primary activity was noting the teachers' responses to and interjections during the facilitator's lecture, the aim being to follow these up during informal discussions with teachers after the completion of the course. Many of the teachers' contributions during the whole-group discussion were recorded verbatim by the researcher. This record was shown to teachers afterwards to verify that it coincided with their recollections of the event.

4   After the course the participants were involved in informal discussions regarding their opinions of its relevance and effectiveness, with particular emphasis on their responses to the theoretical side of CL. Their responses were recorded in the form of notes, with a view to pursue some of the issues raised in the follow-up interviews.

5   Participants who had provided data after the course that seemed useful to the aim of the study were asked for follow-up, taped interviews. These interviews – of much shorter duration than the initial interviews – were conducted under the same circumstances as the initial interviews. The follow-up interviews operated in a more structured way, given that they were primarily reflective of the issues raised in the course. The more formal structure was guided to a large extent by the teachers themselves, who were eager to discuss specific aspects of CL theory as facilitated by the course.

Data analysis

Data collection and analysis were undertaken concurrently in the study. This was due to the emergent nature of much of the data, which required the follow-up of leads and the necessity of allowing the participants to elaborate on issues raised during the semi-structured interviews. The fact that there were to be reflective interviews after the professional development course required the researcher to be familiar with all the data that had been gathered in the initial interviews and during the course, and the dominant themes of the study up to that point had to be established. Another consideration was the masses of information that had been acquired at all stages of the research, which, due to time constraints, also made it necessary to combine the two stages.

Notes made during the initial semi-structured interviews were used as tags for data considered to be particularly useful to later stages of the interviews, and for themes that would be explored during analysis of the transcripts. These notes also tagged data considered to be important for the five criteria of DA (Punch, 1998) – looking for variation, a close reading of detail, looking for rhetorical organisation, accountability and making reference to theoretical texts. After each initial interview the audio tapes were transcribed in full and subjected to the five requirements of DA. All this was done from the perspective of SI theory, which made allowances for the individual circumstances and difficulties of the interviewed participant (appreciative capacity) and enabled the researcher to consider the importance and implications for the study of the participants' own use of language (designatory capacity). The data that resulted were used – without the mention of names – in the interviews with subsequent participants as a means of prompting the elaboration of a variant discourse when it arose in discussion. The leads and conclusions that resulted from each interview were also pursued by further reading, which was incorporated in the analysis process.

After the initial interviews were completed, all the resulting data were 'run open' (Punch, 1998) so that variables and dominant themes might be established. These were recorded for future reference as they emerged during analysis. This resulted in the establishing of provisional discourses, such as that of the anxiety teachers felt at the possibility of an intolerant reaction to CL by their colleagues, and the notion that teachers are the 'tools' of progressive CL theorists.

The next stage was the observation of the professional development course. The provisional discourses, in the form of notes, were annotated as issues were raised that were relevant to them, with the intention of pursuing these issues in follow-up interviews and further reading. A report – with verbatim transcriptions of some of the conversations between the teachers and the facilitator – was written during the course, and was subject to some on-the-spot analysis. This consisted mainly of looking for variation and inconsistencies within individual accounts, and quick comparisons and contrasts between the data provided by individual speakers. A few specific questions (relevant to the guiding questions of the study) were written down as a way of prompting further discussion with teachers. Notes were made of some informal reactions to the course that the participants provided after its completion. All data collected during this observation were then compared with both the provisional discourses/themes that had been formulated, and with the original data gathered in the initial interviews. This resulted in a penultimate collection of major themes on which the reflective interviews acted as a supplement or a commentary. However, any comment in the final interviews that substantially changed aspects of these themes were readily incorporated during the final stage of analysis.

This last stage consisted of not only honing the basic themes that had resulted from all stages of research – essentially, establishing the sort of discourses the teachers were maintaining – but also a close reading of all the data that had been gathered. This was done so that the themes could be verified and other readings of the data could be considered. This last, extremely detailed, stage of analysis was supplemented by re-reading the literature that had proven to be most relevant to the study and by the reading of texts that addressed the main themes that had emerged during research.

To repeat, all stages of the analysis were informed and guided by the five criteria of DA as outlined by Potter and Wetherell (Punch, 1998), with emphasis on the close reading of the data for variations, contradictions and the use of rhetorical language. The assumption at all stages of the analysis was that language tends to operate as socially constructed discourse, subject to variation, but which usually corresponds to social hierarchical structures – i.e. it maintains and perpetuates them. However, the analysis was not only conducted on the data provided by the participants, but also on that provided by CL texts themselves. These texts too were closely read for contradiction, assumption and rhetorical language and the conclusions reached after the analysis were influenced by this close reading, especially the connection between the confusions of teachers and those of the CL texts themselves. The analysis accepted the enormous socio-cultural influence on the making of meaning, and the fact that language often operates as discourses in the service of power At the same time, it was tempered by a liberal-humanist, empathetic perspective as allowed by SI theory. Although the analysis was 'critical' in the CL/cultural studies sense of the word, it did not proceed from the doctrinaire, transcendent and the politically narrow assumptions of much CL literature, which operates as a discourse but has usually not yet been subject to close analysis except by the equally doctrinaire, transcendent and politically narrow Right (see Hirsch, 1996). It may be argued that the analysis outlined here was conflicted in the same way it has been suggested CL theory is, since it combined liberal-humanist and poststructuralist research perspectives. However, unlike much CL theory, the approach outlined here did not assume that strict distinctions between humanisms and poststructuralisms are easily made, or are likely to be made, in English teaching.

Bibliography

Hirsch, E. D. (1996) *The Schools We Need and Why We Don't Have Them.* New York, NY: Doubleday.

Hunter, I. (1994) Four anxieties about English. *Interpretations* 27(3): 1–19.

Lankshear, C. (1997a) Critical Literacy. In: J. Green (ed.), *The Seminar on Cross-Cultural Education: Perspectives on Literacy.* Ed. 270D, Fall 97.

Lankshear, C. (1997b) Language and the new capitalism. *International Journal of Inclusive Education* 1(4): 309–321.

Lankshear, C. and Lawler, M. (1987) *Literacy, Schooling and Revolution.* London: Falmer Press.

Luke, A. (1997) Approaches to the study of literacy and curriculum. In: J. Green (ed.), *The Seminar on Cross-Cultural Education: Perspectives on Literacy.* Ed. 270D, Fall 97.

Macedo, D. (1994) *Literacies of Power: What Americans are not Allowed to Know.* Boulder, CO: Westview Press.

New London Group (1996) A pedagogy of multiliteracies: designing social futures, *Harvard Educational Review* 66(1): 60–91.

Osborne, R. and Van Loon, B. (1996) *Sociology for Beginners.* Cambridge: Icon Books.

Paglia, C. (1992) *Sex, Art and American Culture.* Harmondsworth, Middlesex: Penguin Books.

Punch, K. (1998) *Introduction to Social Research: Qualitative and Quantitative Approaches.* London: Sage.

Rosenbaum, R. (1998) *Explaining Hitler: The Search for the Origins of His Evil.* London: Macmillan.

Steele, M. (1997) *Theorising Textual Subjects: Agency and Oppression.* South Carolina: University of Carolina Press.

Woods, P. (1992) Symbolic interactionism: theory and method. In: M. LeCompte, W. Millroy and J. Priessle (eds), *The Handbook of Qualitative Research in Education.* San Diego, CA: Academic Press Inc., Harcourt Brace and Company.

Chapter 7

Meaning and method

Using metaphors in qualitative research

Helen Wildy

Introduction

I opened the first chapter of my PhD thesis with Greenfield's statement: 'Education is a deeply mysterious process and so is the business of being a leader' (Greenfield, 1984, p. 167). My study dealt with the dilemmas experienced by principals in dealing with the contradictions and pressures of school restructuring. Restructuring here means the move towards school-based management, school-based decision-making, and the community management of schools. I argued that restructuring seeks to improve education by recasting the roles, relationships, and responsibilities of people in schools and central authorities. I aimed to find out what it is about school restructuring that principals find so difficult. The study, conducted in Western Australia in the first decade of state education restructuring, used an emergent research design involving three data sources: descriptions by approximately 1,000 school administrators of cases of principals' work; in-depth interviews with ten principals; and a six-year study of one principal.

Interpretive–constructivist analysis of narrative accounts using actual events recounted in the principal's voice revealed that principals find restructuring difficult because their work is saturated with dilemmas. Three dilemmas were conceptualised: the accountability dilemma that principals are accountable for decisions made by or with others; the autonomy dilemma that principals maintain authority while working collaboratively; and the efficiency dilemma that principals share decision-making while using resources efficiently. Furthermore, principals espouse two opposing clusters of values – caring for and involving others, and strength in making decisions. In practice, decisiveness is a key preoccupation, and participation is a problem for principals. Faced with the untidiness of shared decision-making, principals prefer accountability, autonomy and efficiency over collaboration. This response to the dilemmas is driven by an ethic of responsibility. The meshing of the ethic of responsibility with an ethic of care, however, resolves problems of collaborative decision-making and allows the principal to share accountability, exercise authority and use resources efficiently.

Of the eight chapters in the thesis, the one that I most enjoyed writing was the Methods chapter. Perhaps because I was as interested in *how* I was doing my study as in its substantive issues, I gave this chapter prime place, immediately following the introductory chapter. However, the approach I took in writing this chapter was risky. I could have written it in a conventional way. I could have begun by explaining that I adopted a qualitative research approach. I might have proceeded with a statement of my substantive conceptual framework. The next step might have been to present and justify the method I used to explore principals' experiences of restructuring, and then I would have shown how I constructed narrative accounts of principals at work and described my analytical processes.

However, I chose not to present the Methods chapter in that way. To do so would imply that I had conducted a neat, logical and linear study, twinkling with precision and rigour (Pinar and Reynolds, 1992). Instead, I recounted a story of my dissatisfaction with the quantitative research approach, my flirtation with grounded theory, and my decision to use the narrative account to present my data. Such a research story seemed more appropriate to the story I wanted to tell about school principals' struggle to deal with the dilemmas of restructuring. Moreover, I tried to give an honest account of my methodological journey, which would do more justice to the openness of principals whose stories I presented in the substantive part of my thesis. This chapter is a brief account of that journey.

Exploring restructuring

My awareness of school restructuring was aroused in the early 1980s in the Australian state of Victoria. I was teaching mathematics and studying for a Graduate Diploma of Educational Administration. Having recently arrived from Western Australia and also work in education, I was keen to understand attempts to bring about change through school restructuring. On my return to Western Australia in the late 1980s, in my teaching and studies for a Masters degree in education I was confronted with the impact of the *Better Schools* policy (Western Australian Ministry of Education, 1987); the blueprint for school restructuring in Western Australia.

Early in the 1990s I became interested in principals' perspectives on restructuring. I was contracted to write professional development materials and, subsequently, to present courses to principals over a four-year period in the state education authority's School Leadership Programme. Its aim was to assist principals in adopting the values and practices promoted in the *Better Schools* policy. I expected principals would be eager to involve their staff and community members in school decisions and to share responsibility for school development. However, I was surprised by principals' talk of their sense of powerlessness and the difficulties of increased work and loss of identity (Wildy, 1997; Wildy and Punch, 1997). I felt it was ironic that restructuring was expected to make principals more powerful in their schools and communities but actually left them feeling powerless. This mismatch between what I believed about school restructuring and principals' reports of their experiences of restructuring was the catalyst for my research.

I decided to explore this problem through interview data and field notes collected during my work in the School Leadership Programme. I believed the interviews and field notes allowed me to enter principals' worlds, to see the issues of restructuring as they experienced them, and to understand how they made sense of these experiences.

Conducting the study

My early postgraduate study of statistics and training in experimental research methods had left a deep positivist imprint on me. However, I was becoming less interested in reporting what I presumed to be an objective reality than in the process of constructing meaning. In searching for a more appropriate way to conduct my study, I was attracted to grounded theory.

I read Glaser and Strauss (Glaser and Strauss, 1967; Glaser, 1978, 1992; Strauss, 1987; Strauss and Corbin, 1990). I completed a course on grounded theory and participated in coding seminars with colleagues. I understood that grounded theory had been applied in a range of research areas for nearly 30 years (Punch and Wildy, 1995). It seemed that the grounded theory approach led toward developing theory without reliance on particular lines of research, kinds of data or theoretical interests. It was 'a style of doing qualitative research' (Strauss, 1987, p. 5) whose major feature was a general method of comparative analysis.

The basic tenets of the grounded theory approach appealed to me. First, I liked the distinction between formal and substantive theory (Strauss, 1987, p. 242) and the notion that building knowledge of social phenomena needed theory 'at various levels of generality' (p. 6). I understood that knowledge grew from an accumulation of low-level theory and that, as a researcher, I could contribute one small building block. Second, the grounded theory way of 'discovering' theory (Glaser and Strauss, 1967) seemed to fit with my own beliefs at the time about doing research. In contrast with theory generated by logical deduction from *a priori* assumptions, theory is generated by moving between data and theory, an iterative process that goes on throughout the life of the research. Third is the issue of where the research begins. The grounded theory approach is to start with an empirical problem. Grounded theory does not set out to test hypothesised relationships between known concepts derived from established frameworks. I understood that theory could both reveal and conceal (Eisner, 1988). Reliance on fully developed theory and constructs has both positive and negative aspects. Theory directs and shapes the world we see, focussing our attention on some things and screening out others. Eisner (1993, p. viii) explains the problem in this way: 'The visions that we secure from the theoretical portholes through which we peer also obscure those aspects of the territory they foreclose'. I wanted to understand the sense principals made of their experiences with school restructuring without feeling directed or compelled by preconceived theory or constructs.

A fourth issue is the role of literature in grounded theory. Apart from the initial review of literature to establish the extent to which previous research throws light on the empirical problem, the grounded theory approach incorporates three further uses of the literature (Strauss, 1987). One purpose is to identify emerging concepts and relationships between them. A second use of the literature is as a source of competing theory against which the emerging theory is checked. Finally, the newly generated theory is placed in context with existing relevant theory in the literature. More importantly, though, is the broad definition of the concept of literature. Strauss (1987) advocates the use of a wide variety of sources of literature as data, from exploratory research findings and technical literature within the substantive field and across disciplines, to the researcher's own experiential data. It was the notion of moving backwards and forwards between my data and the literature, broadly defined, that I found attractive because it allowed for my emerging understanding of school restructuring.

Fifth, the grounded theory approach acknowledges the researcher's role in the research process. Rather than acting like an impersonal manipulator of techniques, the researcher can be portrayed as intimately involved in the process, with values, preconceptions, preferences and frailties. I was familiar with the idea of the self as instrument. For example, in data collection the self of the researcher asks questions and interacts with participants. In data analysis, induction is flavoured by the researcher's intuition and intensive first-hand presence (Erickson, 1986).

I followed the debate between the founders of grounded theory (Strauss and Corbin, 1990, 1994; Glaser, 1992) and found myself more sympathetic to the Glaserian version of grounded theory. The debate centres on Glaser's criticism of the Strauss and Corbin interpretation. Glaser is critical of them for representing grounded theory as a set of readily accessible techniques that reveal meaning in data (Glaser, 1992), and argues that meaning in data is generated not by the strategy but by the researcher. In Glaser's view, what Strauss and Corbin advocate is more appropriately named 'full conceptual description' forced from data rather than theory grounded in, and emerging from, data (Glaser, 1992, p. 124). This debate highlighted the role of the researcher, rather than the process, in generating meaning or theory from data.

Finally, the grounded theory approach appealed to me because of its methodological origins. Strauss (1987) describes its development from two streams of thought: the American pragmatism of John Dewey with its emphasis on action and the problematic situation, and the Chicago sociology tradition from the 1920s to the 1950s with its reliance on observations and interviews to grasp the actors' viewpoints and to understand social processes. From this basis comes the connection between grounded theory and symbolic interactionism (Stern, 1994). Of the versions of symbolic interactionism, the one that attempts to make the worlds of lived experience directly accessible to the reader, by capturing the voice, emotions and actions of those studied, is known as the interpretive–constructivist version of interactionism (Denzin, 1992). It was this link between grounded theory, symbolic interactionism and the interpretive–constructivist approach to research that attracted me. And so my first conceptualisation of this study was in terms of grounded theory.

Data collection

The initial formal data collection for my study began with in-depth interviews with ten principals. Initially I used 'convenience' sampling (Cohen and Manion, 1980, p. 76), choosing four principals with whom I had developed special rapport. However, I needed to cover potentially relevant categories such as sex, age, status and location, so I continued my selection of principals using 'quota' sampling (Cohen and Manion, 1980, p. 76). I felt it was important to search for exceptions and to include negative evidence and extreme cases (Denzin, 1978). In the language of grounded theory, this is the process of theoretical sampling in which the researcher seeks *on analytic grounds* what data to collect next and where to find them' (Strauss, 1987, p. 38,) with the goal of maximising variance until no new information is added and 'saturation' of a concept is reached.

Interviews lasted between one and two hours and were unstructured. I knew some of the advantages of unstructured interviews. For example, the unstructured interview gave me opportunities to understand the complexity of principals' behaviour without imposing *a priori* categorisation that might direct and limit the inquiry (Fontana and Frey, 1994). In addition, the unstructured interview allowed principals to speak in their own voices, control the flow of topics and extend their responses (Mishler, 1986). However, there were also disadvantages. For example, because I did not direct the discussion, a range of different issues emerged from each of the interviews. In at least three of the interviews, considerable time was spent on issues that were not relevant to the research topic. Then I began the arduous business of coding the interviews. The transcripts varied in length from 3,500 to 12,000 words. For several years I examined the written texts of field notes and interview transcripts, word by word, phrase by phrase and sentence by sentence. I identified recurring themes, patterns, and ideas. Throughout this period I wrote 'theoretical memos' (Strauss, 1987, p. 109) containing hunches, their modification and refinement, and the linking of concepts into initial attempts at theory.

I was overwhelmed by the volume of analytical material generated by my coding activity. According to Glaser (1992), this is not an uncommon experience for novice grounded theorists who are often 'stumped' by the number of field notes and interviews and the difficulty of pulling together the analysis. By 1995 I had produced two dozen files of theoretical and methodological memos filled with potential theories. One product of this period was a paper about principals' powerlessness (Wildy and Punch, 1997). However, I was unable to synthesise my material, and I too felt powerless and turned my attention to other research activities.

The next part of my story shows how I solved the problem of divergence in my data analysis. In 1996 I embarked on a research project aimed to develop performance standards for school principals (Louden and Wildy, 1999a, 1999b; Wildy and Louden, 2000). The research was based on two premises: one was that performance could be represented in brief narrative accounts or *cases*; the other was the notion of rating performance represented in cases using Item Response Theory, an application of a procedure used extensively in Australia to develop literacy standards (Louden, 1994).

I developed cases depicting a variety of aspects of principals' work from interviews with 74 principals. The interviews, conducted in principals' offices and lasting on average one hour, took place between May 1996 and February 1997. I had a set of possible topics to guide my thinking during the interviews, and I identified five tensions that I had previously noted in principals' talk about their powerlessness:

1   Being a member of a group and also being the boss
2   Being methodical and orderly and also being open to new ideas
3   Responding to centrally imposed regulations and also acting autonomously
4   Having a clear view and also accommodating the views of others
5   Supporting staff while also maintaining standards.

I saw these tensions as dilemmas for principals. Together they constituted a provisional conceptual framework for my thinking about principals' struggle with restructuring.

My custom was to audio tape the interview and write notes, a practice that helped me identify key points later without having to listen to the entire recording. Immediately after each interview I wrote a case based on the interview, and each was returned to the principal for feedback on the accuracy of the representation of the account. In some instances I altered details, such as the school's location or the name of an activity, to ensure anonymity. In a period of six weeks, I wrote 90 cases in this way.

It was my experience writing these cases that provided a solution to the problem of dealing with the divergence of my earlier interview data analysis. In the art and craft of creating a narrative account of a particular issue in a way that had a dramatic tension and was easily read, I became what Eisner (1985, p. 221) calls a *connoisseur*. The connoisseur has the ability to see what is subtle, complex and important, and to place what is seen in an 'intelligible context'. Both 'artistic reconstruction' and 'distillation' are used in writing accounts of what is seen, so that the reader can experience the actions and interactions in a vivid and life-like way. Hence the writer selects some pieces of data and rejects others, retaining both what is enduring and what is particular to create a coherent and persuasive whole.

In my growing connoisseurship lay a solution to my problem of method, namely, how to deal with vast amounts of coded data and theoretical and methodological memoing. Instead of fragmenting the interview data as I had been doing in my grounded theory approach to coding, I had learned a technique to synthesise the interview. Now I had a strategy to reduce a 10,000 word interview into a 1,000 word narrative account. Using the skills I had developed writing a large number of cases from unstructured interviews together with my intimate knowledge of each interview developed from the coding activity, I had a way of dealing with the initial ten interviews. This was a turning point in my study.

At this point, I returned to the literature regarding school restructuring and began to focus on principals' dilemmas of restructuring. I identified three separate dilemmas, and termed them the accountability dilemma, the autonomy dilemma, and the efficiency dilemma. However, these three dilemmas did not come only from the restructuring literature. The dilemmas were derived both from my experiential data – from the School Leadership Programme – and from the technical literature. This is an example of what in grounded theory terms is called 'discovering' theory.

Now I had a strategy for representing my data – writing cases or narrative accounts – and I had identified a conceptual framework for my study. All that remained was to write the thesis. However, to write up what one has discovered is not like uncorking a bottle and pouring out the contents (van Maanen, 1988). There is an art and a craft in the construction of chapters and new decisions are required.

I had to decide which data to include. It seemed that I had data from not one but three sources. First, there was a set of in-depth interviews with ten principals generated from my work in the School Leadership Programme. Second, there was an extensive body of data collected during a six-year case study of Catherine, principal of Waverley High School (both pseudonyms), a rural school engaged in a variety of restructuring activities through its involvement with the National Schools Project. I was interested in how the principal dealt with the tensions of restructuring in her school, particularly on the way she shared decision-making authority but remained a powerful leader in the school and community (Wildy and Wallace, 1997). Third, there were the 90 cases generated from my involvement in developing a standards framework for school principals.

Connecting the data

I had to decide how to connect the data. I linked the three data sources with a metaphor of viewing a statue from different angles and through different lenses. The idea of the statue came from Glaser and Strauss (1965) in their monograph *Awareness of Dying*. In my metaphor, the statue represented principals at work in a restructuring school system. The statue had three faces, representing the three dilemmas of restructuring. Viewing the statue from different angles revealed its different faces, and viewing the statue and its faces through different lenses revealed different meanings or interpretations of the way principals experience the dilemmas of restructuring. The three data sets were the lenses through which the statue is viewed. The experience of Catherine at Waverley High School became a lens through which to explore the dilemmas, the interviews with principals and field notes from the School Leadership Programme formed another lens, and the ratings and descriptions of cases of principals' work in restructured schools constituted a third lens. To distinguish the lenses I used optometric language: a close-up lens, a middle-range lens and a long-distance lens, respectively. Through these three sets of data I explored the main research question: What is it about restructuring that principals find so difficult? In particular, I sought to answer these questions:

- How are the accountability dilemma, the autonomy dilemma and the efficiency dilemma manifest in principals' work?
- How do principals deal with these dilemmas?

The notion of viewing a statue from different angles and through different lenses links to the idea of triangulation (Cohen and Manion, 1980). Talk about triangulation arises in discussions about an inquiry's internal validity or 'truth value' (Guba and Lincoln, 1989, p. 234). The researcher uses multiple methods to overcome the problem of 'method-boundedness' and the subsequent distorted picture of the phenomenon under investigation. This image is the triangle, a two dimensional rigid object providing three sides from which to approach the truth (Denzin, 1978). Indeed, there is assumed to be a fixed point 'out there' – the truth, waiting to be triangulated (Guba and Lincoln, 1989).

However, opinions about triangulation and internal validity vary. For example, in the interpretive–constructivist view reality is a mental construction; there is no reality 'out there' whose truth is to be captured. Instead, reality is constructed by people as they attempt to make sense of their experiences. In this usage, triangulation is the process of using multiple perceptions to clarify meaning, showing the different truths about the phenomenon. Richardson (1994, p. 522) extends this notion by proposing the concept of crystallisation. The image is the crystal, 'combining symmetry and substance with an infinite variety of shapes, substances, transmutations, multi dimensionalities, and angles of approach'. Crystallisation, without losing structure, challenges the traditional interpretation of validity and gives a deepened, more complex, thoroughly partial understanding of the phenomenon. The notion of crystallisation is based on a quite different assumption about truth from the assumption underlying the traditional idea of triangulation. I chose to use a metaphor of viewing a statue from different angles using different lenses, together with the notion of crystallisation, because I knew that the restructuring was experienced variously by individual principals. What the statue looks like depends on the angle of viewing and the lens through which it is viewed.

The three data sources provided three lenses to view the dilemmas of restructuring. The data were generated using quite different perspectives. For example, the standards data were anonymous. Approximately 1,000 principals received cases about unidentified people, either in the mail or in workshop settings. They were asked to rate and describe the performance represented in the cases, and their responses were anonymous. The School Leadership Programme data were obtained from interviews obtained in the privacy of principals' offices. When I wrote the cases based on the interviews, I wanted to show respect for principals' courage in revealing their vulnerability in their reflections to me. The Waverley data came from the study of one principal while I was a guest of the school for six years, visiting the private spaces of the principal's world (Stake, 1994). Catherine is portrayed as a principal whose performance is seamless and whose expertise is invisible. The tone here is celebratory. The three methods provided different perspectives of principals' work in restructured schools. This is how I used the metaphor of viewing through different lenses to crystallise, rather than triangulate, what it was about restructuring that principals found so difficult.

The three data chapters were constructed around cases

depicting principals' work in a restructured school system. Each case was a constructed narrative account, using actual events and the voice of the principal. The accounts were not intended to be iconic images or mirrors of reality (Schwandt, 1994), but rather expressive reconstitutions of the experiences from which they originated (Eisner, 1991).

Data analysis

I had to decide what kind of analysis was appropriate. I chose interpretive analysis because my aim was always to understand the complexities of school restructuring from the actors' point of view, the *emic* perspective (Erickson, 1986). To interpret is to construct a reading of actors' meanings. Schwandt (1994, p. 118) describes the process as preparing 'a construction of the constructions of the actors one studies' However, interpretation is an art that cannot be formalised (Denzin, 1994, p. 504), a 'productive process that sets forth the multiple meanings of an event, object, experience or text'. Interpretation illuminates experience, refining the meanings that can be sifted from the account of the experience. Meaning, interpretation and representation are thus intertwined. My aim in the interpretive analysis of each case was to uncover the theories-in-stories that principals used to make sense of their own world and to show how these theories worked in principals' lives. I adopted a process of 'indwelling' (Eisner, 1981, p. 6), imaginatively participating in the experiences principals recounted. The strategy I used was to ask questions, probing the cases to illuminate aspects of the dilemmas. In my metaphor of viewing a statue, these questions represent adjustments to the viewing position: tilting the head, or leaning from side to side, or moving backwards or forwards, to get a clearer view of an aspect of the statue.

Conclusion

This is my account of the baffling and sometimes mysterious journey I undertook to find out what it is about school restructuring that principals find so difficult. I used a meta-grounded theory approach. I started from an empirical problem, and moved backwards and forwards between my data and the literature to arrive at theoretical constructs, seeking to capture the complex, subtle and shifting meaning that principals created of their experiences of school restructuring. However, I did not develop a grounded theory, with its coalescence of data into a single core category. Instead, I chose the narrative account for data representation, allowing for divergence and richness in capturing the particular and the context of principals' experiences of school restructuring and its dilemmas.

I applied the metaphor of a statue – school restructuring – with three faces; the accountability dilemma, the autonomy dilemma and the efficiency dilemma. These dilemmas are viewed through three lenses: a long-range lens (the standards framework cases and their ratings), a middle-range lens (in-depth interviews with principals), and a close-up lens (a six-year case study of one principal). Rather than attempting to triangulate truth, this approach allowed me to crystallise meaning.

Bibliography

Cohen, L. and Manion, L. (1980) *Research Methods in Education*. London: Croom Helm.

Denzin, N. K. (1978) *The Research Act*. New York, NY: McGraw-Hill.

Denzin, N. K. (1992) *Symbolic Interactionism and Cultural Studies: The Politics of Interpretation*. Oxford: Blackwell.

Denzin, N. K. (1994) The art and politics of interpretation. *In*: N. K. Denzin and Y. S. Lincoln (eds), *Handbook of Qualitative Research*, pp. 500–515. Thousand Oaks, CA: Sage.

Eisner, E. W. (1981) On the differences between scientific and artistic approaches to qualitative research. *Educational Researcher* 10(4): 5–9.

Eisner, E. W. (1985) *The Educational Imagination: On the Design and Evaluation of School Programs*. New York, NY: Macmillan.

Eisner, E. W. (1988) The primacy of experience and the politics of method. *Educational Researcher* 17(5): 15–20.

Eisner, E. W. (1991) *The Enlightened Eye: Qualitative Inquiry and the Enhancement of Educational Practices*. New York, NY: Macmillan.

Eisner, E. W. (1993) Forward. *In*: D. J. Flinders and G. E. Mills (eds), *Theory and Concepts in Qualitative Research: Perspectives From the Field*, pp. vii–ix. New York, NY: Teachers College Press.

Erickson, F. (1986) Qualitative methods in research on teaching. *In*: M. C. Wittrock (ed.), *Handbook of Research on Teaching*, 3rd edn, pp. 119–161. New York, NY: Macmillan.

Fontana, A. and Frey, J. H. (1994) Interviewing: the art of science. *In*: N. K. Denzin and Y. S. Lincoln (eds), *Handbook of Qualitative Research*, pp. 361–376. Thousand Oaks, CA: Sage.

Glaser, B. (1978) *Advances in the Methodology of Grounded Theory: Theoretical Sensitivity*. Mill Valley, CA: Sociology Press.

Glaser, B. (1992) *Basics of Grounded Theory Analysis: Emergence Versus Forcing*. Mill Valley, CA: Sociology Press.

Glaser, B. and Strauss, A. (1965) *Awareness of Dying*. Chicago, IL: Aldine Publishing Co.

Glaser, B. and Strauss, A. (1967) *The Discovery of Grounded Theory: Strategies for Qualitative Research*. Chicago, IL: Aldine Publishing Co.

Greenfield, T. B. (1984) Leaders and schools: willfulness and nonnatural order in organizations. *In*: T. J. Sergiovanni and J. E. Corbally (eds), *Leadership and Organizational Culture: New Perspectives on Administrative Theory and Practice*, pp. 142–169. Chicago, IL: University of Illinois Press.

Guba, E. and Lincoln, Y. S. (1989) *Fourth Generation Evaluation*. Newbury Park, CA: Sage.

Louden, W. (1994) Setting standards in teaching. *In*: L. Ingvarson and R. Chadbourne (eds), *Valuing Teachers' Work: New Directions in Teacher Appraisal*, pp. 96–111. Melbourne: Australian Council for Educational Research.

Louden, W. and Wildy, H. (1999a) Circumstance and proper timing: context and the construction of a standards framework for school principals' performance. *Educational Administration Quarterly* 35(3): 399–422.

Louden, W. and Wildy, H. (1999b) Short shrift to long lists: an alternative approach to the development of performance standards for school principals. *Journal of Educational Administration* 37(2): 99–120.

Mishler, E. G. (1986) *Research Interviewing: Context and Narrative*. Cambridge, MA: Harvard University Press.

Pinar, W. F. and Reynolds, W. M. (1992) Curriculum as Text. *In*: W. F. Pinar and W. M. Reynolds (eds), *Understanding Curriculum as Phenomenological and Deconstructed Text*, pp. 1–14. New York, NY: Teachers College Press.

Punch, K. and Wildy, H. (1995) Grounded theory in educational administration, leadership and change. Paper presented at the Australian Council for Educational Administration International Conference, Sydney.

Richardson, L. (1994) Writing: a method of inquiry. *In*: N. K. Denzin and Y. S. Lincoln (eds), *Handbook of Qualitative Research*, pp. 516–529. Thousand Oaks, CA: Sage.

Schwandt, T. A. (1994) Constructivist interpretivist approaches to human inquiry. *In*: N. K. Denzin and Y. S. Lincoln (eds), *Handbook of Qualitative Research*, pp. 118–137. Thousand Oaks, CA: Sage.

Stake, R. (1994) Case studies. *In*: N. K. Denzin and Y. S. Lincoln (eds), *Handbook of Qualitative Research*, pp. 236–247. Thousand Oaks, CA: Sage.

Stern, P. N. (1994) Eroding grounded theory. *In*: J. M. Morse (ed.), *Critical Issues in Qualitative Research Methods*, pp. 212–223. Thousand Oaks, CA: Sage.

Strauss, A. (1987) *Qualitative Analysis for Social Scientists*. New York, NY: Cambridge University Press.

Strauss, A. and Corbin, J. (1990) *Basics of Qualitative Research: Grounded Theory Procedures and Techniques*. Newbury Park, CA: Sage.

Strauss, A. and Corbin, J. (1994) Grounded theory methodology: an overview. *In*: N. K. Denzin and Y. S. Lincoln (eds), *Handbook of Qualitative Research*, pp. 273–285. Thousand Oaks, CA: Sage.

van Maanen, J. (1988) *Tales of the Field: On Writing Ethnography*. Chicago, IL: University of Chicago Press.

Western Australian Ministry of Education (1987) *Better Schools in Western Australia: A Programme for Improvement*. Perth: Government Printer.

Wildy, H. (1997) Restructuring and Principals' Power: Freedom from Without the Freedom To. Paper presented at the annual meeting of the American Educational Research Association, Chicago.

Wildy, H. and Louden, W. (2000) School restructuring and the dilemmas of principals' work. *Educational Management and Administration* 28(3): 173–184.

Wildy, H. and Punch, K. (1997) The challenges of changing power relations in schools. *In*: B. Conners and T. d'Arbon (eds), *Change, Challenge and Creative Leadership: International Perspectives on Research and Practice*, pp. 95–110. Hawthorn, Victoria: Australian Council for Educational Administration.

Wildy, H. and Wallace, J. (1997) Devolving power in schools: resolving the dilemma of strong and shared leadership. *Leading and Managing* 3(2): 132–147.

Chapter 8

A research narrative

Confronting the tensions of methodological struggle

Tania Aspland

Introduction

My PhD study was initiated in 1993, when I had vested interests in pedagogy and higher education curriculum theorising. At the same time, through my university teaching, I was engaging in pedagogical relations with a number of visiting students from overseas countries. I was continually astounded by the humiliating experiences these students, particularly the women, were enduring in postgraduate courses and higher degree supervision. In a brief pilot study (Aspland and O'Donoghue, 1994) completed in 1992, I was able to determine some key propositions that identified the root of what was problematic in supervision for overseas students in one particular university. What was of greater significance within the pilot study was the recognition on my part, and that of my colleague, of the methodological difficulties we encountered and the failure of our study really to capture what was significant in the postgraduate supervisory experiences for each overseas student. We felt that although the pilot study was worth reporting, we had a lot to learn about methodology and how to move beyond the appearances of supervisory life as described by each student. This demanded that we examine more fully the historically specific and culturally positioned subjectivities that underlie the everyday realities of overseas students immersed in supervisory relations. What we were searching for was a more critical understanding of the life-world (Habermas, 1987) of each student as he or she engaged in supervisory relations in specific university contexts.

Here I report on the evolution of the methodological approaches adopted for a more detailed study with a view to articulating how I confronted the inadequacies of existing research paradigms, particularly from the perspectives of a minority group who continued to struggle within the contexts of higher education. At the outset I want to emphasise that the evolution was anything but rational or linear. Rather, it was a process fraught with intuition, subjectivity and at times confusion, as I stumbled through obstacles, managed research dilemmas and met the challenges of a long-term study that was to become an integral part of the lives of each research participant as well as my own. While some research of this nature can be located quite firmly in one particular research discourse, this is not the case here. In what follows I provide a critique of the range of methodological discourses that impacted on the study as it evolved over three years. Accompanying the critique is an exposition of how I have been positioned as a researcher within the development of the project, and how that positioning has changed with the dynamics of the research.

The creation of a methodological pastiche

What is outlined below is my research narrative of the evolution of a methodological pastiche. I use the word pastiche as I reflect on the methodology since I believe this to be a work of methodological art whereby perceived incongruent forms come together seemingly in opposition (Nicholson, 1990; Lather, 1991), yet ultimately create a research framework that is cohesive. Such cohesion is not indicative of a finite methodological unity; rather, it is a confluence of different research methods that also allows a place for the tensions of ambivalence and struggles that characterise doctoral supervision.

It was (and still is) my belief that a project of this nature could not be locked into one static framework for the duration of such a long-term study. Furthermore, as the shape of the research project transformed with the emerging dialogue amongst the research participants, and the needs of the women in the study changed, so too did the research methods in order better to meet our requirements in light of the research questions. In hindsight, I acknowledge that while I was consciously monitoring the shaping of the research methodology in a systematic and sustained way through the keeping of a research journal, it was at the same time being reshaped from within as the needs of the group necessitated and demanded changing research practices. I am arguing here that the very nature of the research questions demanded this kind of flexibility and open-endedness.

In the beginning

As I entered the study, phenomenology seemed a most appropriate starting point. It was the 'essence' of supervisory experiences that I hoped to gain by investigating the lived experiences of the women in the study. The theoretical constructs of phenomenology provided a platform for me to enter the study and engage in 'authentic' research that I hoped would capture the reality of the politics of supervision for this group of overseas women enrolled in doctoral programmes in three Australian universities. As such, phenomenological research of this type is located within the broader approaches of descriptive and qualitative research. While there is no agreed-upon definition of phenomenology (Patton, 1990), it is generally accepted as the description of particular phenomena that a person experiences.

Phenomenological inquiries focus on the lived reality of participants participating in a research study, and avoid traditional 'scientific' approaches that focus on contrived, collective and objective descriptions of the behaviour of the participants. Thus the philosophical traditions of phenomenology provided the platform for attempting to capture the lived experiences and supervisory relationships for each of a group of overseas women students. I was passionate about capturing these experiences in a way that was ethically honest and representative of the women who participated in the study. As such, I relied a great deal on the day-to-day natural language of the participants in order to report on their lived experiences of doctoral supervision. The study was designed at the outset to 'give voice' to participants set within academia, inviting significant issues to emerge as indicators on which to form the basis of further discussion and research. Data of this sort, I argued, would not be distorted or contrived by predetermined hypotheses or interview constructs that may well have been elicited from the literature. In this sense the present study attempted to make a complete break from traditional research, a field dominated by normative assumptions, conceptual frameworks and methodological tools that, in my estimation, represent faulty reductionist and Eurocentric accounts of supervision.

Historically, phenomenology is a direct reaction to positivism and its obsession with the use of science to explain human behaviour. In this sense, it appealed to me in proposing the original theorising and the methodological framework of the study. Further, as I was intent on capturing the 'essence' of supervisory experiences for each woman, it was to phenomenology that I turned. Central to phenomenology are the schema and frameworks brought into being during the search for essences or essential themes and insights through which the lived experiences are scrutinised (Merleau-Ponty, 1962; Spiegelberg, 1975; van Manen, 1988). It was this richness of the values and meanings inherent in the supervisory experiences of overseas women that my research sought to capture. The phenomenological framework provided a platform to do so. As Schweitzer (1994) argued, phenomenology brings to a study of this type:

> ... a concept of *verstehen*, the 'science' of understanding. The concept of *verstehen* challenges the constructs of *erklären*, the 'science' of explanation, and highlights the subjective nature and richness of the values and meanings underpinning human behaviour as an integral part of the supervisory experiences encountered by overseas students. As such, it acknowledges inner experience, as reflecting the facts of consciousness, as significant.

In pursuing the science of understanding, Husserl (1971) highlighted the importance of everyday phenomena in people's lives – a phenomenon meaning 'that which presents itself' to those who experience it – that is, a lived experience, be it tangible or not. The way in which supervisory meaning is constructed from an individual's stream of consciousness as each participant engages in supervisory relations and tries to make some sense of her daily struggles was central to the early stages of my study as I attempted to unearth the meaning or subjective understandings of supervision for each woman.

It was this focus on the relational nature of everyday experiences that are said to evolve over time and are located in particular social and cultural spaces that contributed significantly to my construction of the initial theoretical framework of the study.

Phenomenology in this sense supported the inclusion in the project of a number of mediating factors, such as space, time and intersubjective understanding, that are central to the shaping of lived experiences of supervision. Mediating factors such as these are absent from the supervision literature. The theoretical framework applied in my study begs the phenomenological question, and a question central to understanding the lived experiences of the participants within this study: 'What is being?' and further, 'What is the nature of "being" supervised?'.

The phenomenological concept of time is an integrated notion that unifies the past, the present and the future as a total entity. Time is a significant construct when considering, for example, each woman's culturally unique and life-long orientation to learning, a concept central to higher degree supervision that has yet to be investigated. Any attempts to dislocate time into its separate components may lead to meaningless and imposed constructs upon the reporting of experiences in ways that are detrimental to the purpose of capturing the sense of 'being supervised'.

The phenomenological concept of time is particularly significant when attempting to converse about particular events and experiences that call on participants to reflect on their lived experiences of supervision and learning as a totality, moving back and forth across past, present and future events. The concept of time continued to be a valuable construct within the study as each woman moved through significant events in her life, her education, her professional work and, in the present context, her supervisory experiences, presenting her socially-constituted self and 'being' through the process of supervision. The phenomenological concept of time is consistent with more contemporary approaches to research that focus on life history (Saunders, 1982; Middleton, 1993) and life stories (Mann, 1992). This approach values subjective perceptions and orientations to events and lived experience by encouraging participants to make connections with the past. In this study, the current meanings and interpretations of higher degree supervision that each woman experiences are shown to have grown and developed over time. In tracing and capturing each woman's history, the study was able to acquire a fuller, deeper and richer understanding of how current experiences were inextricably connected to the past.

By conceptualising this study within the framework of the life-world of overseas women students positioned within supervisory relations, and through investigating the ways in which meaning is constructed and reconstructed as supervisory relations are constituted and reconstituted, the study challenged traditional reductionist perspectives that portray 'the art of supervision' in its technocratic sense, void of contextual issues that constitute intersubjective relations. The impact of phenomenology on this study suggested that supervisory meaning cannot be derived from researching supervisor constructions of 'best practice'. Instead, meaning is derived from the social actors whose life-world the researcher seeks to understand and document. Meaning is made *in situ* and in process as each participant encounters the everyday life and struggles of supervision. Studies of this nature are no longer concerned with the description of a separate realm of being, but rather with the reflection on the description of intersubjective communal experience (Schweitzer, 1994, p. 9). The analytical focus of the study was on the intersubjective experience of 'being supervised', and what each woman interpreted as problematic within those experiences, rather than on the 'problem' of supervision or the 'skill' of supervision. It is the capturing of such intersubjective communal experiences that are particularly important for the phenomenologists because they claim to describe the contradictions, tensions and challenges of lived experiences of supervision from the perspective of the most significant participant, the self.

Too much data?

While my desire to understand how each woman's lived experience of supervision unfolded was an integral component of the study, the phenomenological mode of explication generated large volumes of descriptive data. The aim of phenomenology is description rather than explanation (Ehrich, 1996, p. 198). In this sense the phenomenological approach contributed a great deal to the initial structuring of the research methodologies and practices of this study, and continued to do so throughout the fieldwork during 1993. However, as the first twelve months of fieldwork drew to a close, I became conscious that my research had failed to address *how* each woman's experiences arose within the social relations of supervision. Furthermore, the phenomenological approach failed to place the asymmetrical experiences of supervision in the broader socio-cultural, socio-historical and socio-political contexts emerging at the time in the Australian university sector.

Capturing each woman's lived experience was a central focus of the inquiry. Understanding how that experience unfolded for each woman was an important anticipated outcome, but what became apparent to me was the need to understand how those experiences were socially, culturally and politically constructed in specific contexts. I was keen to address the perceived short-comings of the phenomenological framework by investigating more fully the processes of intersubjective meaning-making that are socially, culturally and politically situated within the super-visory process.

Moving on: the influence of symbolic interactionism

At this point in the research process I turned to symbolic interac-tionism (Blumer, 1969), developed by the Chicago school in the twentieth century. This theory, referred to in the text as SI, seemed to offer the study an orientation that suggested I reshape the research to capture better the social action and meaning-making central to supervision from the perspective of each woman and the contexts within which she is situated.

The three principles central to SI, as formulated by Blumer (1962, p. 2) are applicable in this context. The first principle pro-poses that participants do not simply respond to the stimuli of 'being supervised' as the phenomenologist might suggest; rather, they act towards 'things' (like supervision) on the basis of the meaning that the 'things' have for them. In Blumer's terms, 'things' consist of a broad range of phenomena, from the con-crete (supervisors, policies and universities) to the abstract (situ-ations in which participants may find themselves, such as supervision, and the principles that advise their reaction to inter-actions). Thus participants in a study such as this one should be considered volitional, not simply as participants who respond to supervisory stimuli but as acting participants who cope with, react to and continually constitute and reconstitute particular actions within their settings. In this sense, the meaning-making that is central to supervision forges particular actions for each participant. Of importance here was the realisation for me that, in pursuing the nature of 'being supervised', I had failed to acknowledge the complex processes of meaning-making that were central to supervisory relations.

Blumer's second principle is premised on the proposition that suggests because the everyday relations of supervision call on each participant to interact with others, meaning is granted to the activity of significant others (such as the supervisor) as well as her own. This implies that the meaning of supervision for each participant grows out of the ways in which other persons act towards her with regard to supervision. This jolted me to realise that each participant was 'learning' to reconstitute her supervisory world not simply from 'being supervised' but in response to others with whom she was interacting (i.e. her supervisor, other students, Deans of Faculty, student advisers). These interactions, argue SI theorists, should be central to investigation and analysis. Furthermore, this second principle invites the dynamics of reconstituting relations to be identified as significant to the study, for SI theory deems meaning, not as fixed, but rather as subject to constant readjustment by new information and changing contexts. In other words, each participant acquires meaning from her own supervisory experiences, but because she is in constant engagement with the world and others such meaning is continually being modified and reconstituted in an ongoing manner. The phenomenological focus failed to capture this dynamic.

Blumer (1969) explicates the third principle: 'Meanings are handled, and modified through an interpretive process used by the person in dealing with the things he [sic] encounters'. This implied for me the importance of each participant's interpretation of supervisory encounters and how each woman handled them. Each participant elicits from supervision that which is meaningful. This is then reshaped, responded to, ignored or acted upon in light of how each participant is situated within supervision at any historical moment. Supervisory relations emerge from 'a taking of oneself [self objectification] and others into account' (Meltzer *et al.*, 1975, p. 1).

At the theoretical core of this process of construction is each woman's 'self', which is seen to act as a lens or a filter through which meaning-making is refracted and experienced. Based on my concerns at the close of 1993 it seemed very appropriate to pursue this complementary research pathway, which is 'centrally concerned with [not only] the inner experience of the individual [but also] . . . how the self arises within the social process' (Mead, 1934, pp. 7–8) or, in the case of this study, within the social practices of supervision. My refocussed thinking implied that the reality for each woman was constructed on the basis of the meaning that was made regarding certain constructs within her supervisory world or through social interaction with significant others. Supervisory meaning, in this sense, was not assumed as a given nor as a phenomenon that existed externally to each woman, and therefore was not conceptualised as imposed on that self, as I had assumed previously. This principle negates the belief that the reality of supervision is 'out there' waiting for an individual to claim it, as my work to date had implied. Rather, the reality of supervision from an SI perspective became far more problematic for me as the women's accounts were continually evolving and being reframed, not in isolation but rather as something that was less certain, more emergent and more reflexive in nature. Supervisory meanings were assigned to objects through interaction with others. This was a significant point of transition within the study, when the meanings or experiences being reported by each woman were considered to be socially constituted.

In order fully to understand the socially constituted self underpinning the way in which each woman responded to certain supervisory phenomena, I needed to understand more fully the differing forms of self as espoused by the symbolic interactionist. Initially I focussed on the level of personal interests, beliefs and biography. The way people respond to particular situations, I could now argue, is significantly shaped by their previous experiences and expectations, and the influences of significant others in each person's life. These influences, I soon realised, were the primary forces in shaping how each woman became positioned in supervision, as she coped with the demands of the presenting experiences of university life in a foreign country. During 1993, in my zeal to describe the everyday supervisory experiences of each participant I had failed to recognise the significance of such influences, connections with others, and each woman's history.

On presenting herself to each unique supervisory experience or situation, each woman, I argued, engaged in an ongoing social and cultural process of meaning-making. In doing so, she engaged in personal reflection and subconscious conversations between the personal self, (the 'I') and the social self (the 'Me') as theorised by Mead (1934). The two parts of the self, he argued, are seen to be complementary, the more spontaneous 'I' stimulating overt actions that are then evaluated, reshaped and reconstructed by the regulatory 'Me'. The balance between the two is unique in each social subject in terms of variable dominance of one over the other. Most commonly, however, argues Mead (1934), the 'Me' is more cognisant of and responsive to the reactions and viewpoints of others to the 'I'. The 'Me' represents the habitual and routinised aspects of social life, and is always present, while the more elusive and spontaneous 'I' represents the responsive and situational self.

As the researcher I could never really get to know the 'I' in relation to each woman's supervisory experiences, for it immediately becomes the reflective 'Me' with the completion of an action or a reported action. As Mead asserts, it is only after we have done things that we are going to do that we are aware of what we are doing (Mead, 1934, p. 203). It was the 'Me' in the students' experiences that I had been privy to in the early phases of the study. In the interests of my research questions, I argued at this point, it was the 'I' that I should be pursuing and the interplay of the two selves that was imperative to gain a more thorough understanding of how each woman positioned herself within supervisory interactions.

The SI literature suggests that the interplay of identity, self and role should become particularly significant in pursuing the research questions within the study. With this in mind, I was able to draw the phenomenological essences of experience out of a contextual void. This enabled me to place these experiences within a research framework that valued the complexities inherent in the construction of the 'self' within the multifaceted dimensions of supervision that were emerging in culturally different contexts for each participant. The concept of the reconstituting self became significant in this study because of my enthusiasm to explore why explicit reactions to supervision were reconstructed by each woman in particular ways. It was this conceptual relocating of the self and the repositioning of each woman within supervisory relations (role-making and role-taking) that I deemed worthy of further exploration as I struggled to portray the very complex and differing experiences of doctoral thesis supervision for each woman.

The theoretical framework offered by SI suggests that the responses of each participant within supervision are underpinned by a complex set of beliefs and expectations about, for example, higher degree education, gender-based relationships with others, and supervision and learning. It was these expectations and beliefs – the womens' 'I' – that I hoped to access through the womens' 'Me' that was being presented within supervisory engagements and reported to me. The symbolic interactionist argues that these transformations and dilemmas are responsive to a number of factors, including the interplay between the 'I' and 'Me' domains within the self, together with the reactions of the significant and generalised other within the life-world of each woman. Implicit in the concept of the 'generalised other' is the significance of the relationship between each woman (the self) and the broader values of the society, or relevant social and/or cultural subgroup. The argument here suggests that the factors discussed above do not mould specific relations in a deterministic manner. Rather, through emerging in social, cultural and political supervisory relations, each participant monitors her positioning in light of existing constraints, determining the parameters for the construction of her supervisory experiences. My task, then, was to capture the meanings that permeated the interactions constructed by each woman set within particular social, cultural and political relations at any one point in time.

The relevance of symbolic interactionism for the study located the focus away from exploring thesis supervision as something 'out there' to which students respond, comply or reject. SI provided me with an approach that acknowledged supervision as dynamic. Social relations were not only experienced, but were also continuously shaped and reconstructed by each participant through social discourse with others. Goffman (1983) argues that interactions are not completely independent but coexist with a structural order, each with its own form(s). The two, and possibly others, coexist not in deterministic ways, but in a non-systematically co-influential dynamic. This later work by Goffman offered me an entry point that was missing in my earlier work. It opened up the enquiry to explore in greater depth the situatedness of the supervisory interactions and, for the first time, suggested the significance and place of structural factors within supervision.

I reasoned that it would be methodologically productive to examine further the interplay of intersubjective interactions and the structure–agency nexus within the social, cultural and political relations of supervisory partnerships. Such a challenge invited me to peel back the 'hidden' layers of meaning and reality that lay both laterally across the 'here and now' of supervisory interaction and longitudinally back in time (Woods, 1992, p. 365). I intended to investigate further the intersubjective processes of meaning-making that were carved out of supervisory encounters with significant others. I was keen to investigate the bifurcated images that the women held of themselves as the 'I' and 'Me' became juxtaposed throughout the reconstituting positioning of themselves within supervision. The descriptions that I generated in 1993 had to be reassessed as I confronted where and how 'normative supervisory practices' were breaking down. This theoretical re-conception offered me a way of revelation through disruption (Collins and Makowsky, 1972), not description. SI provided a theoretical framework that captured a unique picture of the dynamics of supervisory encounters for each woman, coupled with how such relations may be related to the broader cultural and social features of a structural order.

The messages emerging from the data collection and analysis during 1994 were enlightening in terms of my original and revised research questions, but only in a partial sense. It became clearly evident that particular power relations emerged within the processes of indication and alignment. Furthermore, the data suggested that each woman became alienated from her supervisor and/or her research work in ways that were disempowering. The interviews revealed that the women were feeling strong emotions of anger and discontent about how they were positioned within supervisory relations, yet each woman assumed that such positioning was typically 'what PhD supervision in Australia was like'. In this sense it was considered 'normal' and, as such, unchallengeable. Each woman considered her struggles to be idiosyncratic and of her own making, within the 'normative' construct of supervision. Towards the end of 1994 it was this sense of 'self blame' that really prompted me to question whether it was the nature of supervisory relations or my methodology that was failing each of my participants.

While the data had been insightful in eliciting the differing ways in which each woman made meaning of her supervisory encounters, and had illustrated the unique ways in which the juxta-positioning of the 'I', the 'Me' and 'significant others' continually reshaped supervisory relations, I soon realised that I had failed to move beyond the 'individualism' that permeated my earlier work in 1993. This work suggested that only individuals exist within supervision. I had failed in my interactions, despite Goffman's references to a 'loose coupling' with broader structural factors, to embed the research in the broader social, cultural and political constructs of university supervision. I continually asked myself, was this a failing of the SI orientation to research, or was it the way in which I had positioned myself as researcher? Or was it both?

More self doubts

These questions recurred as 1994 came to a close, when I really began to believe that my own interests were dominating the study. I had many a sleepless night believing that I was manipulating the data in ways that were exploitive of my participants and yet, at the same time, I knew this was not my intention. My colleagues tried to reassure me that this was a 'natural' phase within a PhD project. One in particular said that the rigour of the SI framework was necessary in a PhD thesis for reliability, validity and consistency. He encouraged me to 'get selfish' and 'push on to finish'. Yet these words brought little relief to my heartfelt concern that my work was little more than 'an ethnographic gaze' (Jordan and Yeomans, 1995) that was not only failing me but was also failing to address the research questions. Most importantly, the study was failing to 'make a difference' in the lives of the research participants.

I began to question my positioning as the researcher within this project. A colleague had once told me that I was racist in my thinking, and these words came back to haunt me. Furthermore, some of the work of bell hooks (1990, 1992) loomed large in my mind, regarding whether an 'Anglo' middle-class academic such as myself could ever be positioned to understand the struggles of overseas women students. The work of Edward Said (1985) had also raised the question in my mind as to whether the research that I had completed was simply another example of research that was shaped by the very colonial thinking and imperialist imposition to which I was vehemently opposed. Was my thinking as an academic and a researcher so deeply defined by the colonialist thinking of my Eurocentric history that I was unable to release myself from its tenacious hold? Was I engaging in the collection of data that upheld imperialist thinking through making statements about it, by teaching it, settling it, ruling over it: in short, engaging in 'Orientalism as a Western style for dominating, restructuring, and having authority over the Orient' (Said, 1985, p. 3). What I was experiencing in my personal research struggle has since been described by Jordan and Yeomans (1995) as feelings and practices that have 'largely ignored or left unanalysed the residual effects of colonialism and imperialism on ethnographic practices in the contemporary period' (Jordan and Yeomans, 1995, p. 390). And so my self doubts continued: Was my thinking so immersed in a colonial ideology (Asad, 1973) as an Australian academic that I felt compelled to maintain my hold over the data and my participants through a 'narrative realism' (Jordan and Yeomans, 1995) that separates the lived realities of the participants from their broader political and cultural settings? Was I engaging in research processes described by Jordan and Yeomans as being 'enmeshed in state forms of power, control and regulation of collective (class, gender, race) and individual identities?' Could it be that I was failing to confront an epistemological standpoint that was simply reproducing more of the same, anchoring my imperial ways of thinking firmly into the research discourse?

It was at this juncture in the study that the nature of the research work completed by critical ethnographers, (Simon and Dippo, 1986; Smith, 1987, 1990; Anderson, 1989) was useful. Their thrust to raise serious questions about the adequacy of interpretative research models in addressing broader issues, particularly those related to the social and cultural reproduction, contributed significantly to the methodological pastiche that was evolving.

Taking another turn: the inspiration of Dorothy Smith

Smith's (1987, 1990) work helped me to open up new ways of looking at things (Greene, 1988). What was required was a methodological reorganisation. I had to relocate myself as the researcher, not outside the research, but where I was actually situated, centrally within the research. Concurrently, Smith's theoretical framework offered me a way to theorise the bifurcated selves that were so central to each woman's supervisory experiences, as well as to my own. I felt confident that Smith's work invited me to move forward, not only in probing the lived realities of a group of overseas women enrolled in doctoral programmes in three Australian universities, but also to do so in ways that revealed the social, cultural and political constructs of their reality.

Smith (1987, 1990) argues that a feminist mode of inquiry must begin with women's experience from women's standpoint and explore how it is shaped in the extended relations of larger social and political relations (Smith, 1987, p. 10). So far I had failed to meet this challenge. I learned this lesson the hard way. Traditionally, such theoretical models of inquiry have been shaped by existing 'extralocal' world views that are implicit in a patriarchal, gender-biased and racist society. As such, Smith argues, they have portrayed women as 'other', theorising social relations as 'extralocal, impersonal, universalised forms of action, . . . the exclusive terrain of men, while women became correspondingly confined to a reduced local sphere of action organised by particularistic relationships' (Smith, 1987, p. 5). I had to place the concept of woman, as the primary organiser of an emerging political discourse, at the centre of research.

Smith's work also facilitated my repositioning as researcher, as woman, and as PhD student within the research project. First, my concerns resonated with Smith's argument that research methodologies such as ethnography are misrepresentative of women's issues in a number of ways because they are shaped by 'relations of ruling'. These, she claims, are deeply immersed in complex sets of objectified and organised practices and a generalised social consciousness (i.e. patriarchy) that are constructed from the standpoint of men who have constituted the ruling apparatus of the most powerful institutions in Western society, universities included.

Furthermore, higher education research (Luke and Gore, 1992; Luke, 1994; Aspland and Brooker, 1998) illustrates quite clearly that women as speakers have had no authority in universities. Women lack any proper title to the construction of knowledge, although they are often complicit in the social practices of their silence (Smith, 1987, pp. 31–34). As a result, women have learned to be partners in trivialising their own subjectivity and experience. We have learned to live inside a discourse that is not ours. This discourse expresses and describes a landscape in which we are alienated, a landscape that preserves alienation as integral to its practice. The research practices in which I was immersed in 1993 and 1994 had done this very thing. Smith (1987, 1990) purports that the everyday world of women is organised by social relations not fully apparent in it nor contained in it, but is impacted by social relations external to it. In my research so far, I had failed to recognise this interplay.

The point of reconstruction for the project as I moved into 1995 had to be at the 'line of fault' (Smith, 1987, 1990) where each woman experienced a sense of incongruence between the reported social forms of consciousness and the reality of her own supervisory world. This disjuncture was staring me in the face throughout the latter part of 1994, as each woman struggled with ongoing supervisory tensions, but I failed to see its significance. This may have been because it was also very much a part of my own supervisory relations within my first supervisory partnership. Like all of the women in the study, I perceived the disjuncture that I, too, was experiencing as a personal inadequacy.

It is essential that this line of fault, now identified, be captured by a living research process (Smith, 1993). To do so invited me, together with my research participants, as a research community, to open up new ways of looking at things. Because we were so deeply immersed in our supervisory relations, we spoke of our experiences as 'insiders'. At the same time we were trivialising our supervisory experiences by failing to see the significance of speaking about our local and practical experiences. What was required of me as the researcher was to rework the research dialogue to examine more comprehensively the incongruences that we were struggling with, and to relocate those experiences in social relations that organise, regulate and determine the various points of contestation inherent in higher degree supervision. To capture this disjuncture was essential, but to go one step further and ask how it is organised, how it is determined, and which social relations generate it (Smith, 1987, p. 50), was the challenge for the redefined project. This was the goal that I was now set to pursue.

In my efforts to rupture the relations of ruling, I had to present to the women participants an opportunity to formulate a new discourse that articulated ways of speaking about our subjectivities politically as well as personally. I realised that much of the pain that I had experienced at the close of 1994 was because I had failed to question the dominant values that underpinned my research practice and theoretical assumptions. What was required of me, together with the other women whose experiences were central to the research, was to make overt many of the assumptions that we had taken for granted and had built into a research discourse 'submerged within an institutionalised and disciplinary identity of its own making' (Said, 1989). It was my responsibility not only to disrupt the existing supervisory struggles that permeated our supervisory relations, but also to disrupt the structure of the research discourse.

Informed by Smith's work, I realised that what I had failed to do was to problematise supervisory relations as central to the research process. By neglecting this, I had been ineffective in theorising the positioning of each woman embedded in the complex social, cultural and political relations of supervision. Further, I was omitting to engage in a dialogue as to how social relations are constructed within supervision, and under what conditions social relations are mediated (Smith, 1987, p. 26). Smith's work advised me that a better entry point to a study of this nature may be found in problematising everyday experience as it is situated materially, socially, culturally and politically.

My quest, then, was to reshape the research dialogue by focussing on how the manifestations of supervisory relations were realised and how the social, cultural and political forms of alienation that we were experiencing emerged as cultural formations within supervision. In problematising our research practices I wanted to explore how we, as a group of women, were positioned in the material and symbolic relations of supervision, how we participated in and contributed to these relations, and how our understandings of these relations worked toward the restructuring of supervision in ways that transformed our ongoing struggles. It became important to explore the politics of supervision, the power relations that we were engaging in between ourselves and our supervisors and, as Middleton (1993) advocates, to recognise that we were constituting such relations as we examined them – never really standing outside them.

In 1995, I set out to refine the research dialogue away from semi-structured interviews towards a dialogue that was immersed in the lived experiences and constitutive actions of our supervisory lives. Dialogical conversation (Herrman, 1982) became for me a more appropriate mode of communication. This was a mode of interaction that was already in place in many respects (for example, before and after the semi-structured interviews), yet until this point I had overlooked its contribution to the research project. The refining of the research dialogue emerged in more naturalistic ways from within the group, and we became the generators of new knowledge as a community of researchers examining our lived supervisory experiences in open and non-restrictive ways.

The emergence of a research community

As a group we met regularly in informal settings, pursuing dialogical conversations (Herrman, 1982) about the complex, contradictory and changing patterns of our supervisory relations, capturing the multiple and contradictory positioning (Nicholson, 1990) that each of us took within supervision. We no longer responded to research questions imposed on the study through my own dominant ideological framework. Questions of this sort had simply distorted the nature of research, furthering the interests of the 'ruling apparatus'.

The pursuit of the problematic within our collective conversations began with a social actuality, an episode, found within the everyday world of our supervisory relations, from which we were able to generate a conceptual argument that was truly representative of our supervisory experiences through the disclosure and explication of its properties. In proposing such a 'conceptual apparatus'(Smith, 1987, 1990) we, as a research community, became more aware that the everyday world of supervision is complex and determined by social, cultural and political relations that are external to and removed from the visibility and control of the participants. By pursuing an investigation that centred on the problematics of locating the subject in her everyday world of higher degree supervision, and by focussing on how everyday experiences are shaped and how they articulate with the larger social, cultural and political constructs that determine the everyday world and higher degree supervision for overseas women students, our research community was better placed to elicit the complexities of lived experiences as the research problem (Smith, 1987).

The research focussed on each of us personally, yet all of us collectively, each woman positioned in differing and evolving relations that determined her experiences as problematic. Our discussions focussed on our simultaneous positioning within supervisory relations as well as the personal experiences, some unique, some shared. As a research community we generated knowledge about our supervisory lives as women and as speaking participants (Middleton, 1993, p. 65). The centrality of lived experiences as a research problematic fostered a more honest and true interplay between each of us as located participants in the generation of a systematic body of knowledge articulating the social relations of the everyday world of higher degree supervision.

From this position, in 1995 we collectively focussed on a commitment to an investigation 'of actual practices and relations' (Smith, 1987, p. 160) and dedicated ourselves to an explication of supervisory relations, how supervision actually is and how 'it' actually works. Of particular significance was the key question: 'How does it happen to me/us as it does?' (Smith, 1987, p. 154).

Repositioning as researcher

In the closing year of the study I felt passionate about becoming more thoroughly immersed in a critical ongoing dialogue with the women in the study. I was intent on making links with emancipatory action through research that was situated in an historically and culturally constructed, institutional context. It was imperative for me to explore more fully the multidimensional world of higher degree supervision – a world that I now realised was not only of biography but also of culture, politics and history (Mac an Ghaill, 1988). This was the void in research that was so blatantly obvious at the close of 1994. From this perspective, the process of intersubjective meaning-making can be appraised as a social, pedagogical and cultural construction that is fraught with political, historically constructed complexities that should be considered far more significantly than I had done to date. To have ignored such complexities placed me in the very position of which I am critical in discussions of the literature – in short, the way I had positioned myself outside the project as researcher had failed to problematise the relationship between myself and the research participant. Thus, the reshaped research practices reflected a more critical orientation that was democratic and empowering in its purposes and intent on capturing the lived experiences of women interacting within the asymmetrical power relations (Quartz, 1992) of supervision.

For the purposes of this study, knowledge was no longer considered simply an outcome of research enterprise but located in the actions of the women who were, through their lived experiences, recreating history. We wanted to create a knowledge 'for us' (Smith, 1987) that more clearly articulated the mediated relations of supervision as we were living them. The key research questions became significant as we explored how we, as marginalised students, were positioned in the material, cultural and symbolic relations of supervision, how we participated in and contributed to these relations, and how our understandings of these relations worked toward the restructuring of supervision in ways that transformed our ongoing struggles.

The emerging shape of the study acknowledged the concepts and lived experiences of power, as well as gender, race and culture, as central to the research constructs of the enquiry due to the very nature of the critical discourse being pursued. My aim was to become more analytically attentive to the historically differing value systems, differing cultural orientations to learning, gender/race/class constructions that underlie the tensions within supervisory communication, and related factors that permeate the asymmetrical power relations implicit in higher degree supervision. During the closing year of the project, 1995, I hoped that our research community would question more thoroughly and examine these relations and cultural constructions with a view to exposing the positioning of the self and the constructs that determined lived experiences of supervision that were located in the particular historically constructed social, cultural and political relations inherent in university culture.

Niggling concerns

Despite my renewed vigour and a sense of theoretical comfort, I was continually conscious of a niggling concern that rendered me feeling like the 'patronising Australian'. The anxiety has been identified by Jordan and Yeomans (1995) in a way that suggests that research orientations such as critical ethnography have their origins in early forms of anthropological research shaped by colonialism and imperialist modes of thinking. As I have stated previously, the issue highlighted by Jordan and Yeomans (1995) was a particularly serious concern for me as the project unfolded. The post-colonial practices of many Australian university staff supervising overseas students became an important theme for investigation, and raised concerns about my own positioning as researcher in a study of this kind. I was anxious to shed my Anglo-Celtic 'links to the functioning of the Empire' (Jordan and Yeomans, 1995, p. 392), and yet at the same time my very presence in the study could well be interpreted as simply another academic submerged within an institutionalised and disciplinary identity of its own making (Said, 1989; Jordan and Yeomans, 1995). It was my intention to pursue Said's (1989) challenge to theorise more completely the problematic of the observer within research, by examining my own epistemological positioning as I attempted to make connections with the participants' lived actualities. I used my research journal to capture the tensions in my thinking and the dilemmas that I faced on a day-to-day basis.

Essentially, in 1995 I had to re-situate myself within the research community so that I was able to disclose what was really happening within our supervisory relationship as we lived it. Up until this point, I had failed to see what Smith has emphasised in her work: 'As thinking heads – as social scientists – we are always inside what we are thinking about; we know it in the first place as insiders' (Smith, 1990, p. 51). By relocating myself within the research community I hoped to be able to engage in conversations with the other women, instead of being on the outside looking in. It required that I give more of myself to the interactions; that I, too, share my struggles and become an active member of the group, not an intruder. I had been loathe to do so in the earlier phases of the study due to the fear of imposing my 'biases' on the study. Some may argue that the concept of 'bias', in a sense, is a modernist anxiety that has no place in a study of this kind. I can see now, in hindsight, that I failed to let go of my 'modernist' historically constructed thinking about scientific objectivism and continually felt 'guilty' about my intervention in the study. My journal reflects an ongoing concern or fear that travelled with me throughout the study to this point. This concern is captured in my recurring question: 'Am I forcing the data?' It was only in the late stages of the study that I released myself from this 'guilt trip' in acknowledging my positioning within (as opposed to outside) the research discourse. As such I no longer felt like the 'missing researcher'; nor did I consider myself an authorial voice (Harding, 1987). Rather, I felt very much at home as 'one of the group'. I came to see myself not as an intruder, but as 'an historically located social subject with specific interests and desires' (Roman, 1992, p. 586), politically and personally engaging in a dialogue about our struggles.

In hindsight, I can report that I found a great deal of comfort in this transition as I was able to release many of the inner tensions of my own supervisory struggles that to this point had not surfaced in a meaningful dialogue with others. While this catharsis may appear to be nothing more than the hermeneutics of self-indulgence to the 'ruling elite', or a simplistic confession (Foucault, 1980) of my inner soul, it did in fact alter the nature of the dialogue in which we engaged. By giving more of myself in the conversations, the disjuncture that we had experienced in earlier interviews in our positioning as researcher and the researched had been ruptured. As a group of PhD students and as women, we were now able to talk about our supervisory experiences with one another in a natural and relaxed manner. The tape recorder disappeared, and my note taking was replaced by a genuine engagement in conversations that became the methodology of the study. Knowledge was generated as we raised each other's consciousness about the differing issues that we found in the tensions and struggles of our supervisory experiences

Success at last?

For the first time in this study, by placing myself where I was really situated (Smith, 1987) our supervisory experiences were made clearly visible. By fracturing the hierarchical relationship that I had covertly put in place for the past two years, we were able to rupture my authority as author and appropriator of other women's supervisory experiences. By interrupting the ethnographic authority I had assumed, which was predominantly self-serving and distorting (Herr and Anderson, 1997, p. 47), I no longer felt guilty of alienating the women from their own stories (Middleton, 1993). I repositioned myself within our research community so that my personal involvement was no longer considered an assumed stance of the 'engaged' researcher; rather, it became a genuine condition under which we came to know each other and admitted one another into our lives (Oakley, 1982, p. 58).

Through this renewed research orientation our 'legitimised' voices (Bakhtin, 1986) were strengthened and articulated as central to the study. I was surprised at how easily these voices came tumbling out (Herr and Anderson, 1997, p. 58) as a result of this reconstruction within the research practices of the study. This raises the question of why it took me so long to come to this point of insight and liberation. I can only speculate that such reflexivity and ideological thinking was covertly restrained by the social relations of the institutional discourse within which I was working. The research world as I knew it was largely organised by institutional relations not fully apparent to me (Smith, 1990), and I had failed to recognise the hold they had over me. What was required of me was a new way of looking at things (Greene, 1988), but I had failed to do this.

Conclusion

In the final months of the project I wanted, with my friends, to generate different types of research practices that recovered really useful knowledge through research (Jordan and Yeomans, 1995). It became our collective vision that our stories, our analysis and our theorising be recognised as a 'dialogical production of a cooperatively evolved polyphonic text' (Packwood and Sikes, 1996, p. 343) that enabled us to investigate and scrutinise the social, cultural and political relations within our supervisory encounters. In doing so, we were able better to facilitate our speaking to ourselves, but also, in speaking to others, overtly recreate ourselves as we spoke.

Bibliography

Anderson, G. (1989) Critical ethnography in education: origins, current status, and new directions. *Review of Educational Research* 59(3): 249–270.

Asad, T. (1973) (ed.) *Anthropology and the Colonial Encounter*. London: Macmillan.

Aspland, T. L. and Brooker, R. (1998) Pathways into postgraduate teaching. *In*: B. Atweh, P. Weeks and S. Kemmis (eds), *Action Research: Partnerships for Educational Change*, pp. 280–301. London: Routledge.

Aspland, T. and O'Donoghue, T. A. (1994) Quality in supervising overseas students? *In*: O. Zuber-Skerritt and Y. Ryan (eds), *Quality in Postgraduate Education*, pp. 59–76. London: Kogan Page.

Bahktin, M. (1986) Speech genres. *In*: V. W. McGee, C. Emerson and M. Holoquist (eds), *Speech Genres and Other Late Essays*, pp. 377–408. Austin, TX: University of Texas Press.

Blumer, H. (1962) Society as symbolic interaction. *In*: A. M. Rose (ed.), *Human Behaviour and Social Processes*, pp. 179–192. London: Routledge and Kegan Paul.

Blumer, H. (1969) *Symbolic Interactionism: Perspective and Method*. Chicago, IL: University of Chicago Press.

Carr, W. and Kemmis, S. (1986) *Becoming Critical: Education, Knowledge and Action Research*. London: Falmer Press.

Collins, R. and Makowsky, M. (1972) *The Discovery of Society*. New York, NY: Random House.

Ehrich, L. C. (1996) The difficulties of using phenomenology: a novice researcher's experience. *In*: P. Willis and B. Neville (eds), *Qualitative Research in Adult Education*, pp. 197–214. Victoria: David Lovell Publishing.

Foucault, M. (1980) *Power/Knowledge: Selected Interviews and Other Writings, 1972–1977*. New York, NY: Pantheon Books.

Goffman, E. (1983) The interaction order. *American Sociological Review* 48: 1–17.

Greene, M. (1988) *The Dialectic of Freedom*. New York, NY: Teachers' College Press.

Habermas, J. (1987) *Theory of Communicative Action, Vol. 1, Reason and the Rationalisation of Society*. Boston, MA: Beacon.

Harding, S. (1987) (ed.) *Feminism and Methodology*. Bloomington, IN: Indiana University Press.

Herr, K. and Anderson, G. (1997) The cultural politics of identity: student narratives from two Mexican secondary schools. *Qualitative Studies in Education* 10(1): 45–61.

Herrman, A. (1982) *The Dialogical and Difference*. New York, NY: Columbia University Press.

hooks, b. (1990) *Yearning: Race, Gender and Cultural Politics*. Boston, MA: South End Press.

hooks, b. (1992) *Black Looks: Race and Representation*. Boston, MA: South End Press.

Husserl, E. (1971) Phenomenology. *The British Society for Phenomenology* 2(2): 77–90.

Jordan, S. and Yeomans, D. (1995) Critical ethnography: problems in contemporary theory and practice. *British Journal of Sociology* 16(3): 389–408.

Lather, P. (1986) Research as praxis. *Harvard Educational Review* 56(3): 257–277.

Lather, P. (1991) *Feminist Research in Education: Within/Against*. Geelong: Deakin University Press.

Luke, C. (1994) Women in the academy: the politics of speech and silence. *British Journal of Sociology of Education* 15(2): 211–230.

Luke, C. and Gore, J. (1992) Women in the academy: strategies, struggles and survival. *In*: C. Luke and J. Gore (eds), *Feminism and Critical Pedagogy*, pp. 192–210. New York, NY: Routledge.

Mac an Ghaill, M. (1988) *Young, Gifted and Black*. Milton Keynes: Open University Press.

Mann, S. J. (1992) Telling a life story: issues for research. *Management Education and Development* 23(3): 271–280.

Mead, G. H. (1934) *Mind, Self and Society*. Chicago, IL: University of Chicago Press.

Meltzer, B., Petras, J. and Reynolds, L. (1975) *Symbolic Interactionism*. London: Routledge.

Merleau-Ponty, M. (1962) *Phenomenology of Perception*. London: Routledge and Kegan Paul.

Middleton, S. (1993) *Educating Feminists: Life Histories and Pedagogy*. New York, NY: Teachers College Press.

Nicholson, L. (1990) *Feminism/Postmodernism*. New York, NY: Routledge.

Oakley, A. (1982) Interviewing women. *In*: H. Roberts (ed.), *Doing Feminist Research*, pp. 30–61. London: Routledge and Kogan Paul.

Packwood, A. and Sykes, P. (1996) Adopting a postmodern approach to research. *Qualitative Studies in Education* 9(3): 335–345.

Patton, M. J. (1990) *Qualitative Evaluation and Research Methods*, 2nd edn. Newbury Park: Sage Publications.

Quartz, R. (1992) On critical ethnography. *In*: M. LeCompte, W. Millroy and J. Preissle (eds), *The Handbook of Qualitative Research in Education*, pp. 448–505. San Diego, CA: Academic Press.

Roman, L. (1992) The political significance of other ways of narrating ethnography: a feminist materialist approach. *In*: M. LeCompte, W. Milroy and J. Preissle (eds), *The Handbook of Qualitative Research in*

Education, pp. 555–594. San Diego, CA: Academic Press Incorporated, HBJ Publishers.

Said, E. (1985) *Orientalism*. London: Penguin.

Said, E. (1989) Representing the colonised: anthropology's interlocutors. *Critical Enquiry* 15: 205–255.

Saunders, P. (1982) Phenomenology: a new way of viewing organisational research. *Academy of Management Review* 7(3): 353–360.

Schweitzer, R. (1994) Philosophical foundations of phenomenology. Paper presented to Phenomenography Interest Group, Brisbane: Queensland University of Technology.

Simon, R. and Dippo, D. (1986) On critical ethnographic work. *Anthropology and Education Quarterly* 17(4): 195–202.

Smith, D. E. (1987) *The Everyday World as Problematic: A Feminist Sociology*. Boston, MA: Northeastern University Press.

Smith, D. E. (1990) *The Conceptual Practices of Power: A Feminist Sociology of Knowledge*. Boston, MA: Northeastern University Press.

Smith, R. (1993) Potentials for empowerment in critical action research. *Australian Educational Researcher* 20(2): 75–93.

Spiegelberg, H. (1975) *Doing Phenomenology: Essays on and in Phenomenology*. The Hague: Martinus Nijhoff.

Tisher, R. and Weedon, M. (1990) *Research in Teacher Education: International Perspectives*. London: Falmer Press.

van Mannen, J. (1988) *Tales of the Field: On Writing Ethnography*. Chicago, IL: University of Chicago Press.

Walker, R. (1985) *Doing Research: A Handbook for Teachers*. London: Methuen.

Woods, P. (1992) Symbolic interactionism: theory and method. *In*: M. D. LeCompte, W. L. Milroy and J. Preissle (eds), *The Handbook of Qualitative Research in Education*, pp. 337–404. San Diego, CA: Academic Press Incorporated.

Chapter 9

Reflections on a social semiotic approach to discourse analysis in educational research

Anne Chapman

Introduction

The term 'discourse analysis' is used diversely in educational research as both a methodological framework and a method of analysis. In either case, it embodies multiple approaches that share a general concern for the construction of meanings in, primarily, classroom discourses. More particularly, discourse analysis 'focusses attention on the way language is used, what it is used for, and the social context in which it is used' (Punch, 1998, p. 226). This chapter illustrates an approach to discourse analysis based on the theory of social semiotics. This particular approach is best understood as a methodology in that it provides a theoretical framework for the analytical methods it embodies.

The methodology was used in my PhD study, which identified a recent trend in perspectives on the study of language and mathematics away from early constructivist-oriented approaches towards a concern with the social interactive nature of meaning and learning. Following this trend, a theoretical framework based on social semiotics was developed to argue that mathematical meanings are constructed in part through specific language practices and formations. Moreover, it was argued that learning mathematics requires transformational shifts between 'less mathematical' language and 'more mathematical' language. The empirical investigation provided a descriptive account of the language practices characteristic of school mathematics. Multiple transformational shifts between less mathematical language and more mathematical language were found to be a dominant feature. Transformational strategies of the teacher, and student responses, were identified, and a model was proposed where mathematical meanings are constructed within the shift towards increasingly mathematical language.

The research approach used in the study was developed at the 'point of need'. A review of the literature identified a range of perspectives on the study of language and mathematics, classified under the headings of constructivism, social construction of meaning, mathematical discourse and the language arts movement. It was found that the different theoretical perspectives share a concern with four key factors in mathematics learning: cognitive, linguistic, social and contextual. The need, then, was to develop a theoretical framework that integrates these factors, a methodological position in line with that framework, and appropriate methods of data collection and analysis.

It was considered that a social semiotic perspective on language and mathematics could be seen to pull together the common threads of the various perspectives. Social semiotics is a theory of meaning that focusses on social interaction; on how people construct systems of meaning. It allows an understanding of both language and other systems as semiotic resource systems – that is, systems of possible ways of meaning (Chapman, 1997). Importantly for research in the context of classroom education, it considers too that language operates together with other semiotic systems, such as mathematics, to produce the meanings of a learning area.

An analytical approach based on the principles of social semiotics was developed to take account of the subject specificity of school mathematics discourse. This new approach serves two purposes: first, it establishes a fundamental principle of social semiotics, namely, that meanings are always produced in context; second, it adds a new dimension to understandings of social semiotic theory in order to account for the perceived shifts between 'non-mathematical' and 'mathematical' language. This was a major challenge, since no practical guidelines existed to provide direction. It was also pioneering as it necessitated drawing upon a number of diverse positions, thus shifting the boundaries and creating a new analytical technique.

The following sections of the chapter draw on the data, analytical techniques and findings of the study of spoken language practices in school mathematics to introduce and demonstrate key aspects of the analytical technique. Specifically, the study was an investigation of the spoken language of the teacher and learners in a Year 9 Australian government school mathematics class over a ten-week school term (Chapman, 1997). The main aim of the study was to identify and analyse the language practices of school mathematics discourse.

From the social semiotic perspective taken, school learning areas are social practices in which teachers and learners use language, together with other semiotic systems, to make meanings. Within this perspective, discourse analysis is employed in this chapter to examine the uses of language in terms of two semiotic formations, activity structures and thematic structures, to show how meaning is produced in context. The analysis develops the idea that meaning can never be understood outside of social action.

The analytical terms and techniques follow Lemke's account of how language is used to 'control social interaction and present the meaning relations of the subject' (Lemke, 1985, p. 2). Lemke's approach provides a useful way to describe how, within a language register, activity structures and thematic systems combine to produce a discourse. My concern in this chapter is with illustrating an analysis of the way language makes sense in part through the context in which it is produced. 'Doing' mathematics in school involves acting, speaking and meaning in particular ways. The chapter aims to illustrate through discourse analysis the importance and complexities of situational context in meaning production in school mathematics.

The chapter begins with an account of its analytical terms. It then goes on to analyse the texts of two episodes of classroom talk from a single mathematics lesson on the topic of 'factorising'. Both episodes involve dialogue between the teacher and individual students, and perhaps can best be described as 'teacher-led discussion'. The analyses build an overview of the language strategies used across episodes to negotiate and develop the interactional and thematic patterns of the lesson. They show how the mathematics content of the lesson is contextualised by the interactional functions of language – that is, how the teacher and learners use language to structure both the routines and the thematic meanings of the lesson.

Language, theme and interaction

In examining the discourse of the science classroom, Lemke has identified two important functions of language; 'the coordination and control of what we do and when, and the control and development of our use of the *thematic systems* of science' (Lemke, 1982, p. 264). The first function refers to the interactional context of the situation, the second to the thematic context of the situation. Everything that is said or done in a particular situation can be assigned a meaning in, and contributes to the development of, both of these contexts. They are thus interdependent.

Following Halliday's (1978) model of language as a semiotic resource, Lemke introduces a distinction between two kinds of semiotic formations, namely, activity structures and thematic formations (Lemke, 1987, p. 219):

> Every meaningful action in the classroom makes sense as part of some recurring semiotic pattern. It belongs to one or more semiotic formations. These can be described in two ways: as *activity structures*, recurring functional sequences of actions, and as *thematic formations*, which are recurring patterns of semantic relations among the themes and concepts of a particular way of speaking about a subject.

Activity structures, then, are regularly repeated and socially recognisable sequences of actions. They are distinct patterns of actions that have a beginning and an end. The activity structure itself is recognisable and repeatable, although its action types and sequences may vary on different occasions. Some common activity structures of classroom lessons are the 'homework review', 'small-group discussion' and 'teacher demonstration'. Different mathematics lessons on different topics comprise the same kinds of activity structures. For example, they might all begin with a session on 'mental arithmetic', followed by a 'homework review', and 'whole-class discussion'. Activity structures comprise smaller parts: action types such as 'teacher question', 'student answer', and 'teacher evaluation'.

Different sequences of action types can constitute the same activity structure. Consider a worked example of a standard written algorithm by the teacher of a mathematics lesson. This activity structure can be realised in a number of different ways: through questioning individual students to elicit the 'correct' method, writing a formula on the blackboard, or presenting numerous examples. All of these sequences result in the same activity structure, the 'worked example'. Activity structures are the routines of classroom interaction. Mathematics classrooms generally exhibit the same sorts of activity structures from lesson to lesson, and from topic to topic.

Thematic structures are the systems of relations among themes. Discourse analysis of thematic structure considers how the language of a text is used to develop themes, and also to relate themes to each other. Texts about similar concepts are said to share the same thematic system. Thematic systems can be identified at a number of different levels: the broad themes of a whole curriculum, topics from lesson to lesson, and topics within a lesson. At the narrowest level, relationships among the meanings of individual words are used in constructing meanings and developing themes.

The following analysis of Text One is in two stages. The first is an examination of the interaction strategies of a regular classroom activity to see how language is used to build the patterns of the activity structure; the second is an examination of how language functions to develop the thematic content of the lesson *within* the context of this activity structure.

Text one

1	Teacher:	I want to start with something called factors. Could you write
2		down the heading and the date? Let's make some progress. Is
3		anyone particularly cold in here? Do we need this heater on, or
4		are we OK? You're cold, are you? I'll turn it on for a little while.
5		OK. Put the heading up, please, and then just stop and think for
6		a couple of minutes. Think about what it means. Can anyone tell
7		me what factors are? Now don't hide. Don't avoid it, face it,
8		because in this lesson we are going to go quite a long way in terms
9		of skills. We are going to reach right back to about Stage Two
10		and right up to Stage Four, where we are now. So try and sort of
11		stay for the ride. We need to start by getting a clear idea on
12		what we think factors are. What do you think, Justin?
13	Justin:	Numbers that go into one another.
14	Teacher:	Numbers that go ... Give me an example.
15	Justin:	Like two goes into eight. Four goes into eight.
16	Teacher:	So what are you saying?
17	Justin:	Two and four are multiples of –
18	Teacher:	Two and four are factors of eight. Exactly right. Exactly so. Now,
19		you're all clear on that idea? Scott, is that your idea of what
20		factors was?
21	Scott:	What?
22	Teacher:	What he said.

23	Scott:	What did he say?
24	Teacher:	Did he not say it loud enough? Try again, Justin.
25	Justin:	If you've got the number eight, the factors of eight would be one,
26		two, four, so they go into eight, so that you know the –
27	Teacher:	Is that your idea of what factors are?
28	Scott:	Yeah.
29	Teacher:	Tell me a number *not* a factor of eight.
30	Scott:	Three.
31	Teacher:	OK. And you're all happy about the ones that are? Alright,
32		factors are a pretty simple idea. The actual word I want to work
33		on right now is something that builds on that. It's the word
34		'factorise'. Does anyone know what factorise means?
35	Ian:	Sort of like, umm, for eight to factorise you sort of take the
36		numbers out of it.
37	Teacher:	Give me an example.
38	Ian:	Umm.
39	Teacher:	I like what you've said, but it's not clear to me.
40	Ian:	Umm, the factorise of eight is four times two, or something.
41	Teacher:	Spot on. Exactly so. To factorise a number you turn it into factors.
42		So here's eight. Now if I was to turn that into factors, I've got to
43		turn it into things that multiply to give eight. In other words, to
44		factorise that, I'll do it right now, and I'll use Ian's example,
45		four times two. But that's not the only way to factorise eight.
46		Would you like to write that down and then factorise eight a
47		different way? Yes, Linda, pardon?
48	Linda:	Eight times one.
49	Teacher:	Eight times one is eight factorised. Good. Write down all the
50		ways to factorise eight. Just try it. Think about it for a few
51		moments. Don't tell me about it yet. OK. Can anyone talk it back
52		to me? Come on, give me something. You're all talking amongst
53		yourselves. Tell me, Ashleigh.
54	Ashleigh:	You want another one?
55	Teacher:	Yes.
56	Ashleigh:	Two times four times one.
57	Teacher:	Two times four times one. Is he right?
58	Students	Yes.
59	Teacher:	Yes, you can't say he's wrong. He's written eight as a set of factors.
60		Yes, that's factorised. Yep.
61	Thomas:	One times one times one times two times four.
62	Teacher:	One times one times one times two times four. Can't say he's
63		wrong, again. Yeah, yeah, OK. Yes, there's a lot isn't there?
64		Keep going. Nobody said this to me. What about this? Is sixteen
65		eight factorised?
66	Students:	No.
67	Teacher:	Sorry?
68	Thomas:	Sixteen isn't a factor of eight.
69	Teacher:	Why not?
70	Thomas:	It's a multiple.
71	Teacher:	OK. Good. Alright, so sixteen's got larger. How did we, put your
72		hand up, please. I want to actually see you rather than just have
73		you call. How did we describe a factor previously? Somebody
74		described it here and, umm, you're right. Sixteen's cut out. Why?

75	Linda:	It's a number that will go into another number.
76	Teacher:	OK. Is half a factor of eight?
77	Students:	Yes.
78	Astra:	'Cause it's multiplied by sixteen.
79	Teacher:	How did you describe a factor originally? I mean, I say no it's
80		not, because I remember another word that's part of the way we
81		described it.
82	Kim:	It's whole.
83	Teacher:	No, the word wasn't whole. The word was ... What's an
84		important word that comes up quite a lot. Yes, Stuart?
85	Stuart:	I was going to say it was a multiple, a multiple of that.
86	Teacher:	Sixteen's a multiple. Half's a factor.
87	Stuart:	The factor is a multiple of eight.
88	Teacher:	Could someone, I don't want to spend much more time on this,
89		could someone just tell me, I'm saying half is not, why isn't a
90		half?
91	Stuart:	'Cause directly you have to multiply it by sixteen.
92	Teacher:	OK. So you have to multiply it by sixteen, and sixteen ... OK.
93		That's one way of looking at it. How did we describe it? Jared,
94		tell me what a factor is.
95	Jared:	A factor is something that can be timesed by another number to
96		get –
97	Teacher:	So, a half could be timesed by something to get eight.
98	Jared:	– Well.
99	Teacher:	– I like what you're saying, but there is a nicer way of saying it.
100		Somebody said it earlier.
101	David:	If two numbers can be multiplied together to another number then
102		they are both factors of that number.
103	Teacher:	So sixteen and a half are both factors, are they?
104	Student:	Yeah, some of them.
105	Teacher:	You're saying yes now. The way you described it. Yet I want it to
106		be known as it happens, I don't want sixteen to be a factor. We
107		don't believe it is, anyway. What's, how do you sort it out, yes?
108	Arthur:	Well I think it is because a half times two times two times four
109		is a factor of eight.
110	Teacher:	Anyone want to solve the problem for me? I don't want that to be
111		an example. I want a way of getting out of it. There is a simple
112		way.
113	David:	It has to be a whole number.
114	Teacher:	You could say that. It has to be a whole number. I mean, I believe
115		it has to be a whole number. In fact, the way it was first described
116		made it have to be a whole number because whoever said it,
117		maybe I'm only dreaming somebody said it, but I'm sure
118		somebody said a factor is a number which does what?
119	Jared:	Divides by –
120	Teacher:	Divides, divides equally. That's right. What does divide
121		equally mean? No halves. No bits left over. So I think that
122		definition is nice because it cuts out this idea and forces it back to
123		these ones.

Language and interactional control

The above text is taken from the opening part of the lesson. It is typical of all teacher-led discussions in this class. The students appear to be familiar with the routines of the activity and know its regular patterns. There is a clear pattern in which the teacher introduces the theme of the discussion, then conducts a series of dialogues with individual students in order to develop the thematic content. Any dialogue among students is mediated by the teacher. The boundaries of the episode are determined by its theme: factors – actually a sub-theme of the main topic of the overall lesson, factorising.

In this text, the teacher is clearly the authority in terms of organising the structure and assessing the value and correctness of an answer. He is in apparent control of the discussion, prompting students to provide examples and asking them to clarify and elaborate on their answers. In lines 71–72, for example, the teacher's role is reaffirmed by reminding students to put their hands up. This is said almost as an aside in the middle of a question about how to describe factors.

How is language used by the teacher to negotiate and develop the activity structure? At the beginning of the lesson, the teacher includes himself as a participant in the activity; 'We are going to ... (line 9), 'We need to start by getting a clear idea on what we think factors are' (lines 11–12), 'How did we describe a factor ...?' (line 73). In contrast, there are many more cases in which he treats the students as a group apart from himself, for example, 'you're all clear on that idea?' (line 19), 'you're all happy about the ones that are?' (line 31), drawing on individuals to talk through their own ideas. This power relation highlights the teacher's authority to control and regulate the discussion and to assess students' answers. The students concur with these power roles, responding hesitantly in most cases when prompted by the teacher to give examples and clarify their statements.

The teacher's opening statement, that he is starting with 'something called factors', suggests that this is not the central topic of the lesson. What is to follow (simplifying) is not mentioned in this episode at all. The following instruction to write down the heading (factors) and the date is a signal for the lesson to begin. This is the regular opening activity pattern for this class; the teacher states the topic, instructs the class to prepare for work, the students rule up a page, the teacher chats ('Do we need the heater on, you're cold are you?').

The question 'Can anyone tell me what factors are?' (lines 6–7) is not just a direct question eliciting a direct response. Rather, it functions as an implication that this is something that the students should already know. There is no disapproval, however, of those who do not know or cannot remember what factors are. In fact, in the next few lines the teacher establishes that the whole group, including himself, is going to 'face' this task of understanding factors. Words like this suggest that it will not be easy, that they will do it together, implying at the same time that it is alright not to remember topics from Stage Two. 'We need to start by getting a clear idea on what we think factors are' (lines 11–12) serves two immediate purposes: first, it establishes the group, 'we'; second, it spells out that the task at hand is to provide a definition of factors.

The teacher asks Justin what he thinks factors are. Justin does not volunteer an answer, but is chosen by the teacher and, by the rules of this class, is required to respond. Asking Justin what he *thinks* factors are, and not *what* factors are, gives him a number of options. He is not required to provide a specific answer. Justin does, in fact, have an answer: a phrase typical of mathematics classrooms, 'Numbers that go into one another' (line 13). It is not unusual to use this kind of language to talk about division. The teacher does not ask Justin to rephrase or elaborate on the answer, but to provide an example of what he means. Justin's example shows that he has a clear understanding of his own description of factors. The teacher's next question leads Justin towards a more formal and standard definition. Justin produces the required structure, but says the word 'multiples' instead of 'factors'. He apparently associates factors with multiples, presumably from Stage Two. His understandings of multiples and factors, and the relation between them, are not explored at this stage. In fact, the teacher interrupts Justin's response, 'Two and four are multiples of –' (line 17), restating it as 'Two and four are *factors* of eight (line 18). The teacher has cut off Justin's response, ignoring the word 'multiples' altogether. He follows up the new statement, 'Two and four are *factors* of eight', with a strong, positive emphasis on this being the 'right' idea (line 18).

The interaction with Justin, set up by the teacher, is abruptly halted. A new interaction is initiated with Scott. The immediate function here is to rebuke Scott for not paying attention. It also allows the idea about factors provided by Justin to be reiterated and explored further. Scott provides a contrasting theme, 'what is *not* a factor of eight', which is used to close this part of the episode.

The teacher then introduces a new theme, factorising, following the same pattern. He asks a student what the word 'factorise' means, asks for an example, then expands on that example. He calls on several students to provide examples of different ways to factorise eight. Eventually, he provides a 'problem', in the form of a non-example. This begins an episode in which students are required to find an explanation for why sixteen and one half are not factors of eight. This part of the text involves greater student response and a presentation of ideas. The discussion becomes repetitive and the teacher leads the students towards the required answer quite explicitly.

Language and thematic development

Having seen how language is used to create the situational context of Text One, the following thematic analysis explores how language is also used to create and develop mathematical meanings. Consider first the kinds of words used. Among the words used to build the activity structures are the many topic-specific words and phrases that reflect the theme: factors, numbers, go into, multiples, factorise, multiply, times by, factor of, whole number, divides by, divides equally. The students tend to 'mathematise' the language they bring with them to the classroom, so that they develop a hybrid language comprising phrases and statements such as 'go into', 'factorise means take numbers out of it', 'the factorise of eight', 'sixteen's got larger', 'the factor is a multiple', 'timesed by' and 'multiplied together to another number'. Typical phrases or clauses in the text that tie terms together can be identified: ... are factors of ..., the factors of ... are ..., ... factorised is ...

These students are using both 'natural' (or everyday) and 'mathematical' language to talk about mathematics in a way that makes sense to them. There is a definite shift from what, at this stage, can be described as non-mathematical to mathematical language, as more 'technical' terms are taken up. The grammatical structure also reflects this shift, as recognisably mathematical forms are modelled and repeated. Some examples of this style are 'numbers that go into one another', 'factors of', 'multiply to give', 'factorise something (number)', 'eight times one is eight factorised' and 'eight as a set of factors'.

The text also shows the relations of the meanings of words to one another. It is these relations that are used to develop thematic systems and to construct the meanings of mathematics. The first such relation is provided by Justin: factors link numbers of certain kinds. For example, two and four are factors of eight. The teacher uses Justin's example with the number eight to set up a contrast, or opposition (line 29). The implication here is that, if we know what a factor is, then we also know what a factor is not. The teacher uses Justin's answer of three being a number *not* a factor of eight to reiterate this contrast and effectively end this part of the discussion (line 31).

A new thematic development takes place in lines 31–34. The new topic-word is 'factorise'. The teacher states that this builds on the idea of factors. Another student, Ian, offers his own understanding (lines 35–36). He uses the word factorise, but with a hesitant, non-mathematical description.

In lines 41–47, the teacher elaborates on Ian's example. He suggests that he understands what Ian means, but that it needs to be stated more clearly – that is, in more appropriate or precise language, perhaps. Ian's example is not particularly cogent, but contains the essential elements of a 'correct' answer: 'factorise' and 'eight is four times two' (line 40). Once again, the teacher restates the student's answers in the appropriate style of language. Ian's 'for eight to factorise, you sort of take the numbers out of it' (lines 35–36) is restated by the teacher as 'To factorise a number you turn it into factors' (line 41), and Ian's 'the factorise of eight is four times two' (line 40) becomes 'I've got to turn it (eight) into things that multiply to give eight' (lines 42–43).

An important part of this restatement is the part of speech. Ian uses the word 'factorise' as a noun ('the factorise of eight') in line 40. This misuse of the part of speech is not explicitly mentioned, but the teacher displays its use as a verb four times in this example. This 'restating' is a recurring technique in this and most other lessons for this class. It serves to model the appropriate language style and use.

An important aspect of the thematic relations of the lesson, the link between the words 'factor' and 'factorise', is also developed in this part of the text. Factorising a number is turning it into factors. This links back to the earlier part of the lesson, which deals with factors. Linda makes this link (line 48), drawing on a previous example.

In line 49, the teacher introduces the passive transformation: 'Eight times one is eight factorised'. This provides a model of yet another way of *using* the word factorise. While none of the students actually use this form in this extract, it fits closely with the ways in which they talk about factors and numbers generally, using terms such as 'timesed by' and 'multiplied by'.'What about this?' (line 64) refers to '$8 = 16 \times 1/_2$', written on the blackboard by the teacher. Once again a contrast is produced, this time between 'eight factorised' and 'eight not factorised'. This introduces a third phase of the thematic development of the lesson, the topic of multiples. The word 'multiple' was used, albeit wrongly, by Justin (line 17) earlier in the lesson, and this was ignored by the teacher. No mention was made that it was, or would become, relevant to the lesson. Another student, Thomas, brings up the word 'multiple' in line 70, which this time, rather than being dismissed and passed over, is regarded as 'good'. In order to develop this new theme, the description of factors is called up again, together with the new contrasting relationship between factors and multiples. The idea of multiples is not really explored. The teacher has agreed that sixteen is a multiple of eight, without explaining what this means. The message here is that the numbers in question are either factors or multiples. Any further relation is not considered. There is clearly a connection, but what it is is not stated explicitly.

Thomas's comments (lines 68 and 70) that sixteen is not a factor of eight because it is a multiple initiates a lengthy discussion, leading to a new definition of factors. The previous description, things that multiply to give a number, is no longer sufficient, because by that definition sixteen *is* a factor. A type of game ensues, as students are asked to put forward reasons why sixteen and one half 'cut out', or are not factors of eight. The teacher asks for a word to provide the explanation. Kim suggests the word 'whole' (line 82). The teacher replies 'No, the word wasn't whole' (line 83), with no explanation of why this word will not suffice. In fact, in the following transcript from an episode following Text One, the word 'whole' is used in just this way:

Teacher: OK. Can you have some different numbers. What about two and a half and two? Don't two and a half and two multiply to give five?

Student: Yes, but that half –

Teacher: That's right, yes. We're dealing with whole numbers. That's always been the assumption. OK.

In Text One, Stuart (line 87) makes the statement 'The factor is a multiple of eight'. This seemingly nonsensical statement actually makes use of the contrast between factors and multiples, and produces a possible thematic relation between the two. Based on what he knows to be true from the discussion so far, there is no reason why a factor cannot be a multiple. (Indeed, eight *is* both a factor and a multiple of eight.) Stuart's statement is not followed up, however.

The teacher leaves this discussion and points out that one half is not a factor of eight (line 89) and that he doesn't *want* sixteen to be a factor (line 106). The idea of multiples is not further discussed. His statement that 'We don't believe it (sixteen) is (a factor), anyway' (lines 106–107) is challenged by Arthur, who provides an example typical of those used previously in this lesson to describe factors. It also deals with the teacher's problem of not wanting sixteen to be a factor of eight, by splitting it into its own factors. This is not the answer that the teacher wants, however. He is still searching for the key word. This word is 'equally'. The teacher states that there was an earlier description of factors as numbers which divide equally. (In fact, this term was not used earlier in this lesson.) A new definition of factors is introduced, and this episode ends. The only explanation of what divides equally means is 'no halves, no bits left over' (line 121). This is quite a complex concept, given the themes covered so far, and there is no evidence that the students agree with the teacher that the definition is 'nice' (line 122).

Text One involves several dialogic relationships between teacher and students. Each separate dialogue helps develop the thematic meanings of the lesson in some way. For example, Justin is chosen to represent the kinds of ideas that the students have about factors. The teacher leads him by asking questions. Scott is asked a question because he is not paying attention. This is also used to develop the thematic content of the lesson, repeating and elaborating on Justin's answer, and also to provide a contrast: that is, a number *not* a factor of eight.

A clear pattern that emerges is for the teacher to ask a question, one student answers (either volunteers or is selected by the teacher), then the teacher follows this up by requesting a specific example. A second pattern is to set up contrasts: for example, factors/not factors and factors/multiples. Two interruptions to these patterns are glossed over or ignored. Stuart tries out an idea (line 87) that does not seem to make sense and is not dealt with. Arthur challenges the teacher's assertion that 'we don't believe sixteen is factor of eight'. The teacher overrides this (lines 110–112) and again does not address the logic of the answer.

The teacher refers back to the definition of factors several times, although in the final part of this extract he provides a new definition. Overall, the thematic connections among factors, factorising and multiples are tied together by the definition of factors and by the extended use of the one example (factors of eight). The teacher ensures that the themes and topics of the dialogue – factors, factorising and multiples – are closely related, largely by using the same example to explore all the themes. He constantly refers to what was said earlier, and builds on other dialogues and answers.

It appears that the participants of this episode are on the whole successfully communicating with each other about the meaning of factors and factorising. The teacher implies that he knows what Justin means, and that the misuse of the word multiples is not important. Justin's explanation to Scott clarifies and expands on his previous answer, suggesting that he is communicating well with the teacher. Scott provides only one example of a number not a factor of eight, so it is difficult to assess his meaning. Ian's explanation of factorising is brief and hesitant. The teacher again implies that he knows what the student is trying to say, and elaborates at some length without further response from Ian. Several other students provide examples of how to factorise eight, but there is no real dialogue on the implications of finding several sets of factors. The teacher assumes that the students understand this idea, but there is no lengthy student discussion to validate this.

The discussion of whether sixteen and one half are factors of eight provides a stronger response from students and allows them to talk through their ideas. Students introduce the words 'multiple' and 'whole', and Stuart presents the case that a factor is (could be) a multiple of eight. The question asked in lines 89–90 is *why* one half is not a factor of eight, which results in several students responding. The answers given show that the students share an understanding of the original definition of factors (lines 61, 75–78, 95–96, 101–102, 108–109).

There are a number of ways in which the teacher and students use language structures to construct meanings – that is, to make sense with one another. The teacher's main strategy is to suggest that *he* knows what each student means and to get students to elaborate or provide an example for the benefit of others. Often this involves restating a student's answer in more formal mathematical language. In this episode, it has been shown, this involves grammatical structure as much as the kinds of words used. The students cooperate by answering the teacher's questions and incorporating the language modelled by the teacher into their responses. Justin's example of factors is 'Like two goes into eight, four goes into eight' (line 15). The teacher's response begins 'Two and four are factors of eight' (line 18). Justin later states 'the factors of eight would be' (line 25).

There is no indication here that the *students* are communicating with one another. The teacher acts as mediator in any student interaction. All communication is between the teacher and a student, or between the teacher and the class.

The kinds of meanings being shared are about mathematical terms and processes. There is evidence of shared meanings about 'factors of numbers being numbers that multiply together to give that number'. This is displayed several times. The teacher's meaning about factors dividing equally is not developed and may not be shared by students. The teacher sets up a situation in which the students are searching for the word that is apparently the key to the meaning. In fact, the idea of dividing equally is not discussed further in this lesson and it is not at all clear what meanings the students have made of this notion.

The students who speak in this episode appear to understand what the mathematical terms mean. Even where language is used inappropriately, the teacher models the 'correct' usage and students pick up on this very quickly. The mathematical language used is not particularly complex, and concerns grammatical structure more than terminology. Phrases such as 'timesed by' and 'go into' are acceptable in this class and are even used by the teacher (line 97) to make a point.

There are several instances where students may be in doubt about the meanings of the language used. Ian's answer in lines 35–36 certainly appears correct to someone who knows how to factorise (the teacher), but it is not at all clear that Ian has the same understanding as the teacher. He provides only one example, and it is the teacher who points out there are other ways to factorise eight. Stuart may be in doubt about the relationship between factors and multiples (line 87). He appears to be talking through an idea, but this is not followed through. Finally, Arthur's opinion (lines 108–109) is backed up with an example. The teacher states that he does not *want* this to be an example, and it is interesting that Arthur does not argue his case. It is possible that he makes a new meaning or sees a flaw in his idea.

Text two

1	Teacher:	Righto, would anyone like to talk to the class about factorising
2		this one? Alright, Ryan, you were going to say, tell us what you
3		were going to say, again. Come out to the board in fact and do it.
4		Right, can you give Ryan a couple of minutes of your time,
5		please?
6	Ryan:	I thought, seeing that we are trying to go back in exactly the
7		opposite direction, we should do exactly the opposite to what's
8		there. X squared is equal to x times x so I did x divided by x and
9		then because there's a plus five, I did minus five, all heading
10		back in the other direction and five x, oh, five, because that's
11		five times x you do five divided by x and plus six is negative six.
12	Teacher:	Anyone say anything about that? Positive, negative, good, bad,
13		interesting, awful, what? Umm, Jared. So what's your answer,
14		Ryan?
15	Ryan:	That is, that is factorised to that.
16	Teacher:	OK. Sit down.
17	Ryan:	It's very complicated.
18	Teacher:	Now, factorise. Here's the acid test. Here's the test that shows
19		if that's the right answer. What can I do to check that it's the
20		right answer?
21	Linda:	Work it out.
22	Teacher:	What do you mean, work it out?
23	Linda:	Multiply it.
24	Teacher:	Multiply it back again. Now let's try it. X divided by x. What's
25		x divided by x?
26	Astra:	Zero, zero.
27	Linda:	One, one.
28	Teacher:	It happens to be one. Take five. What's one take five?

29	Students:	Four.
30	Teacher:	Negative four divided by x. What's negative four divided by x?
31	Students:	Negative four x.
32	Teacher:	It happens to be, the best I can do is negative four over x, take
33		six. Does that look like where we started?
34	Students:	No.
35	Teacher:	Which is, in fact, that. No, right, I'll tell you another reason
36		why it's not right, because when we're, over here I gave you four
37		x plus eight y and I said factorise it. You didn't say, well, that's
38		four times x, so I'm going to do four divide by x and that was that
39		plus that. You didn't think that way, did you? You didn't think
40		that way over here. There's not really a good reason for thinking
41		that way over here. No, not really. The best I could use for that
42		is interesting as someone over here once said, but not right. Could
43		anyone come through with . . . alright, Ian. Right, let's hear
44		what Ian's got to say.
45	Ian:	Umm, well, do the same as what you were doing over there. Y, or
46		with these you have to, you draw a little table over here, umm,
47		that add to the five, add to the five and times to give six, and
48		you get two and three, and there's a x squared, so it's got to be
49		something like two plus x times brackets three plus x.
50	Teacher:	Fascinating. You certainly pulled in a little bit of stuff there
51		that we haven't been talking about. Is he right? How can we
52		know he's right?
53	Students:	Work it out.
54	Teacher:	You're right. Have you done this unit before? Alright, let me, let
55		me give it the real test, and if you multiply it you get the right
56		answer. I'll do it very quickly, 'cause I can be quick at this. Two
57		times three is six. That's the outside two. That's the first two,
58		outside two. Two times x is plus two x, inside two x times three,
59		plus three x, last two x times x plus x squared. Now have a look
60		at that. I see an x squared. An x squared. I see a six and a six plus
61		two x plus five x, so it's certainly right. Now whatever he's done
62		he's produced the right answer. What he has done is used a few
63		tricks that may have not been completely clear to you. Can
64		anyone explain it without kind of, this is good, I like this over
65		here, but I don't want to talk about it especially yet. Could
66		anyone explain what's going on without that? Just quickly.
67		Stuart.
68	Stuart:	Oh, I just thought that x squared is x times x, so in front of the
69		brackets it has to be x times x, first two –
70	Teacher:	Can I write that down?
71	Stuart:	Yes.
72	Teacher:	What, do you know it's going to be two brackets, do you?
73	Stuart:	Yeah.
74	Teacher:	How do you know?
75	Stuart:	Because we've been learning it.
76	Teacher:	Alright, it's like the other one, so we're expecting two brackets.
77	Stuart:	You're going to have, because it's x squared, it's x times x, the
78		first two –
79	Teacher:	You're happy with that?
80	Students:	Yeah.

81	Teacher:	'Course, yes.
82	Stuart:	And then you're going to have two numbers that join together to
83		make five.
84	Teacher:	Why?
85	Stuart:	Well, 'cause the second, the outside two, has to add up to five,
86		'cause that's what's in the first set, so –
87	Teacher:	Kelly, do you believe that or do you think he's, do you think
88		he's right? Are you saying that 'cause he's usually right, or
89		what? OK. David?
90	David:	You've got to have two numbers which add to make five and
91		multiply to make six. You've got to have those two numbers, you
92		can't –
93	Teacher:	Hold it, please. Stop, you're running ahead of Stuart. I wanted to
94		talk about, are you all happy with Stuart's idea that you need
95		two numbers to add together to make five?
96	Students:	Yes.
97	Teacher:	Why do you need two numbers to add to five? Could someone tell
98		me in simple terms? Yes?
99	Stuart:	Because there's a plus five x.
100	Teacher:	Let me just do something different. When I multiplied this out I
101		got x squared. If I had used the formula completely, I would
102		have had x squared. What's the outside two?
103	Students:	Three x.
104	Teacher:	Plus three x, the inside two, plus two x and the last two.
105	Stuart:	Two plus six.
106	Teacher:	Three x and two x become five x. OK. And now we can see where
107		the ... OK. We need two numbers that add to five. Yes, Stuart?
108	Stuart:	But the two numbers also have to multiply to six, because when
109		the, umm, last pair, when they're together and they both have
110		to multiply to six, so two numbers that do that are two and three,
111		so then it's x add, because there's adds in the first one, you've got
112		to do add two and the add three. Can you get that answer to just
113		that end one?
114	Teacher:	What one?
115	Stuart:	Can you write that complete factorised thing up there, x times
116		two and x times –
117	Teacher:	You mean the multiplied thing, x squared plus five x plus six?
118	Stuart:	Yeah. Is it easier the way you worked it out? You have a look at
119		the two of them, they're exactly the same. You know, which
120		means that the two things have to be exactly the same, you just
121		swap them around.

The analysis of Text One showed how the mathematics content of the lesson is contextualised by the interactional functions of language. What is said and what is meant depends largely on the context, or the nature of the activity. Text Two is the transcript of another episode from the same lesson. However, the following analysis does not consider the interactional and thematic functions of language in turn. Rather, it explores them together in order to see more clearly how language is used to structure the routines of the mathematics classroom and, *at the same time*, construct the thematic meanings of the lesson.

'Righto' instructs the students to stop talking and pay attention to the teacher. It introduces a new episode in the lesson, in which students are going to 'talk through' their factorising strategies to the rest of the class. Ryan is chosen as the first to do this. Whereas earlier he was stopped from presenting his ideas, he is now invited to speak. Ryan adopts the style and tone of language usually used by the teacher when explaining the workings of a problem to the class. He refers to the class as a whole as 'we', stating the problem (seeing that we are trying to . . . '; line 6) and then the method of solution ('we should do' . . . ; line 7).

Again Ryan states his assumption that factorising is the opposite to multiplication (lines 6–8). This time, however, this assumption is not queried by the teacher. Ryan makes the logical connection that 'we should do exactly the opposite to what's there'. The mathematical content of the expression written on the blackboard is referred to for the first time here. 'What's there' refers to the expression $x^2 + 5x + 6$. 'Do' refers to the arithmetic operation to be applied to each element of the expression. Ryan isolates the separate elements and applies what he considers the appropriate operation to each. He does apply the inverse operation in each case successfully. While he deals with each element separately, his final answer is given as one expression, $x - x - 5 - x - 6$. He has made some important mathematical meanings about inverse operations and about positive and negative numbers. He apparently has some definite ideas about the relation between factorising and multiplying, and seems to be working towards realising them in a mathematical process. His progress is constrained by the pattern of the activity structure, which is for Ryan to wait now for the teacher's appraisal of his response.

The teacher does not immediately assess Ryan's answer himself, but asks the class what they think. Receiving no response, he asks Ryan, 'So what's your answer?' (line 13). Ryan takes up this opportunity to further clarify and summarise his explanation. He uses the 'mathematical' style of language often modelled by the teacher to point out that 'that ($x^2 + 5x + 6$) is factorised to that ($x - x - 5 - x - 6$)'. The original expression and Ryan's answer are both written on the blackboard, and he points to each in turn. The teacher instructs Ryan to sit down, effectively stopping any chance of elaborating further. Ryan interjects with 'It's very complicated' (line 17), perhaps as an excuse if the answer isn't correct, or as a defence for an inadequate explanation.

The teacher again invokes the factorise/multiply relationship, ostensibly to check whether Ryan's answer is correct, but also as a pedagogic task. His questions force the students to use the appropriate words. 'Work it out' is not an adequate answer. Asked what this means, Linda responds 'Multiply it'. The teacher repeats this, but adding 'back again' (line 24). The meaning that multiplication is the inverse of factorising is being further developed here. To check whether the expression has been factorised, you not only multiply, you multiply *back again*. The constant referral to the factorise/multiply contrast is now realised explicitly, using Ryan's answer.

In multiplying out Ryan's answer, the teacher deals with the expression as a whole, which Ryan did not do. The teacher's multiplication clearly shows that Ryan had not factorised the original expression, because multiplying it out (the inverse) does not give that expression. The teacher gives a further explanation of why Ryan's approach is not correct. He refers to an earlier example, $4x + 8y$, and the way that was dealt with. He points out that the students did not deal with the $4x$ separately. The implication here is that no problems should be dealt with in this way. Therefore, Ryan's approach must be wrong. He describes Ryan's approach as 'interesting', but what this means is not clear. More specifically, it is 'not right' (lines 42). Ryan does not defend his answer. In all interactions of this nature, where a student presents a possible answer or approach, the teacher assesses it as right or wrong. A wrong answer typically ends the interaction with the student in question, and another is invited to put forward his or her ideas.

Ian puts his hand up, volunteering to present his method of factorising the expression, which he does in lines 45–49. Ian presents a clear, concise and 'correct' account of how to factorise the expression. He demonstrates the process on the blackboard, drawing up a mathematical table and talking through the steps. He writes his answer, $(2 + x)(3 + x)$, on the blackboard. He has apparently learned his procedure previously and understands its mechanics. The teacher describes the method as fascinating, but does not yet assess it as right or wrong. Again, the teacher asks the students how they can find out if this answer is correct. This time, when the class responds in chorus 'Work it out' (line 53), the teacher does insist that they use the word multiply. 'You're right, have you done this unit before?' (line 54) he asks of the class as a whole, not just Ian. It is clear now that many students share the meaning that 'working it out' means to 'multiply back'. The teacher reiterates this in lines 54–56.

In lines 56–66, the teacher simplifies Ian's answer and determines that it is correct. He says that he will do this very quickly, which he does, talking through each step. As he talks, he uses the terms 'first two', 'outside two', 'inside two x' and 'last two x'. This is the first time he has used these terms. It seems at this stage that he is gradually going to introduce an algorithm, after using its terms in conversation. In fact, a specific algorithm is not mentioned until much later in the lesson. However, in line 101, the teacher states, 'If I had used the *formula* completely, I would have had ... ' (my emphasis). This suggests that the teacher assumes that the students already know the formula to which he is referring. The fact that no-one questions the teacher about this 'formula' suggests that he may be right. So a lengthy exchange is built around the assumption that many students already share the teacher's meanings about how to factorise.

Returning to lines 62–63, the thematic meanings of the episode are clearly both enabled and constrained by the structures of the routine. The teacher suggests that Ian has used a few 'tricks'. He points out that he likes 'this' (the table drawn by Ian on the blackboard), but doesn't want to talk about it yet. In fact, the table is not mentioned again in this lesson. Stuart, who produced an incorrect answer to this problem earlier in the episode, is now invited to explain 'what's going on' in Ian's method. But Stuart has further developed his own meanings about factorising and multiplying and has approached the problem somewhat differently to Ian. Ian's answer is now left behind as the teacher works through Stuart's own ideas, step by step, writing each stage on the blackboard.

Stuart knows what the answer will look like; it will have two sets of brackets, with a binomial expression in each. The teacher asks how he knows this, and Stuart points out that it is 'Because we've been learning it' (line 75). The teacher accepts this answer, which effectively maintains focus on the current theme. It is now expected that all problems will have an answer with two sets of brackets. This is typical of this and many other mathematics lessons for this class; one type and form of problem forms the basis of the whole lesson. Students realise this pattern and predict what their answers should look like.

Stuart explains how he arrives at the elements in the brackets. David interrupts the teacher to clarify this explanation, restating Stuart's remarks in more concise, 'mathematical' language – 'numbers that join together to make five' (lines 82–83) is restated as 'numbers which add to make five' (line 90). David starts to explain the method of factorising being developed, but is cut off by the teacher, who wants to take it more slowly. 'You're running ahead of Stuart' (line 93) serves two immediate purposes. First, it implies that David is correct, and second that the discussion will eventually get to the point already reached by David. He returns to Stuart's example, referring to the process mentioned as 'Stuart's idea'. At this point it seems that many students do know this method of factorising, and probably the implied algorithm, too. This is evident in the exchanges in lines 108–121. The students who speak seem to want to move more quickly. The teacher is still focusing on the term $5x$, while students introduce the last term, 6. The students already know the connection between these terms, as demonstrated by David (lines 90–91) and Stuart, who actually interrupts the teacher to point out that 'the two numbers also have to multiply to six' (line 108). His explanation is disjointed and much less clear than David's. The language is less 'sophisticated'. For example, he calls positive numbers 'adds'. However, he has apparently made the same meanings as David.

Finally, Stuart asks the teacher to write the 'complete factorised thing' on the blackboard (line 115). The teacher corrects him: 'You mean the multiplied thing' (line 117) and rewrites the original expression. Stuart raises a new point: whether the two different factorisations on the blackboard, his own answer, $(x + 2)(x + 3)$, and Ian's, $(2 + x)(3 + x)$, mean the same thing. He understands that they do and that there are different ways of arriving at the answer. This provides a new sub-theme, which is developed in later parts of the lesson.

Analytical findings

This chapter has examined instances of discursive semiotic formations in a mathematics lesson. The analysis has sought to show, through limited examples, that the meanings of school mathematics are always produced in context, and cannot be understood outside of the social practices of the classroom.

The texts analysed share similarities in the patterns of their activity structures as well as a unifying set of themes and subthemes. Text One was examined in two stages, considering first the interactional and then the thematic development. The activity and thematic structures of Text Two were then considered together in order to show more clearly the nature of their integration.

The interactional pattern evident in these episodes is to introduce the theme and then conduct a series of dialogues with individual students. The thematic content is developed within these dialogues. Activity structures are centred around one problem or example, written on the blackboard, which is used to develop the theme. The teacher is the authority, the 'holder of knowledge', and determines whether an answer is correct. This power relation is central to negotiating the activity structure. The teacher controls and structures the discussion by questioning students, often drawing on their knowledge by directing them to elaborate or clarify their answers.

In Text One, this power relation is not immediately obvious. For example, early in the discussion the teacher uses the term 'we', including himself as a participant in the learning task. Students are asked what they think and are encouraged to present their ideas. In the ensuing dialogues, however, the teacher refines these ideas and directs them quite explicitly towards the 'correct' meanings. In Text Two, it is apparent that many students are already familiar with the thematic content and that the teacher is constraining the meanings put forward by several students.

Language is used to generate meanings in a number of ways in the lesson from which these texts are drawn. There is a clear shift away from 'everyday' or non-mathematical language towards what has been described here as mathematical language. The dominant strategy for affecting this shift is teacher re-wording of student language to include topic-specific words and phrases. The particular grammatical structure of mathematical language is also modelled. The relations of words to one another, notably contrasting words, are emphasised, as are the different meanings that some words have in different contexts. The shift towards mathematical language does not happen here as a linear progression. Rather, these texts show a phase of 'hybrid' language use in which students try out different aspects of the mathematics register, adopting the language style modelled by the teacher and incorporating it into their own ways of speaking. The teacher too moves back and forth judiciously between non-mathematical and mathematical language in order to build up the thematic patterns of the lesson.

This brief discourse analysis illustrates how language has been used by the teacher and students to build the regular patterns of mathematics classroom activity and, within a familiar classroom activity structure, develop the thematic systems, or mathematical content, of a lesson. The analysis shows that language use contributes to both these structures simultaneously; language is used to structure the routines of the mathematics classroom and, at the same time, construct the thematic meanings of the lesson.

Conclusion

This chapter has illustrated, through the use of transcript data, a new social semiotic approach to discourse analysis in educational research. Drawing on a study of school mathematics discourse, this innovative approach has been used to examine the role of language in the thematic and interactional development of mathematics lessons. It has identified language practices characteristic of school mathematics and has highlighted some specific ways in which these practices enable meaning construction. It has established too that language is used by teachers and learners both to structure the routines and to construct the thematics of a lesson. The social construction of meanings through language use is a key concern for both researchers and educators. Discourse analysis is a significant and germane development in this regard.

Bibliography

Chapman, A. P. (1997) Towards a model of language shifts in mathematics learning. *Mathematics Education Research Journal* 9(2): 152–173.

Halliday, M. A. K. (1978) *Language as Social Semiotic*. London: Edward Arnold.

Lemke, J. L. (1982) *Classroom Communication of Science*. (Final report to the US National Science Foundation.) Arlington, VA: ERIC Documents Reproduction Service No. ED 222 346.

Lemke, J. L. (1985) *Using Language in the Classroom*. Geelong, Victoria: Deakin University Press.

Lemke, J. L. (1987) Social semiotics and science education. *The American Journal of Semiotics* 5(2): 217–232.

Punch, K. F. (1998) *Introduction to Social Research: Quantitative and Qualitative Approaches*. London: Sage.

Chapter 10

The route less travelled

Reflections on research for the PhD by publication

Anthony Potts

Introduction

This chapter is a critical commentary on the research that resulted in the writing of my book *College Academics* (Potts, 1997) and an abridged version of a thesis that, with the book, comprised my PhD (by publication) submission. In a review of *College Academics* Tight (1999, p. 128) noted its lack of a personal perspective. Following this, he asked me whether I might be in a position to write a paper on the research for the book, the production of the book and how it was received'. In similar vein, Theobald (1998, p. 29) asks her readers how they would respond to an invitation to talk *about* their work rather than *from* their work; to talk about the intellectual passions that kept them going when they felt like giving up. Tight's (1999) and Theobald's (1998) observations have influenced the following chapter.

College Academics

College Academics (Potts, 1997) is a study of the world of academic staff undertaken by an inside researcher. The focus is the occupational socialisation of academic staff at one of Australia's oldest Colleges of Advanced Education. *College Academics* examines how staff from the Schools of Business, Science, Engineering, and Arts learnt the skills, attitudes and values that helped them adapt to their occupational world. The chief interests of study were the perspectives of the academic staff.

The timeframe is the period 1965 to 1982. This period witnessed strong growth in the whole higher education system in Australia, followed by drastic restructuring and curtailment of growth. Thus the work is an historical investigation, with implications for academic careers, careers in general and wider issues of higher education policy.

College Academics utilises socialisation theory from the Chicago School of Symbolic Interactionism. The methods used in the study were those of life history. Intensive interviews with 53 full-time academic staff, supplemented with documentary analysis and participant and non-participant observation, were used in the study.

The book focusses on the following themes: obtaining a position as an academic, perspectives on working as an academic, perspectives on teaching and research, and perspectives on commitment. Of particular interest is the relative influence of academics' own tertiary education, previous employment, the effects of working in a College of Advanced Education, and the importance of significant others in an academic's world. Also of importance is how these academics responded to working in a tightly controlled government institution set up to achieve specific economic and educational aims.

Context issues

Origins

Discovering why I undertook the writing of *College Academics* is an interesting issue. Berger (1963, p. 12) observes that a benevolent interest in people could be a starting point, but he also cautions that a malevolent and misanthropic outlook can provide motivation. I am hoping that in my case there was more of the former. Woods (1996, p. 1) notes that 'personal realities' are important in research but may be hidden, and he suggests that these can be more important for the choice and direction of the research and for the researcher. He notes that one may do research partly to discover oneself, and that it is chiefly through the self that the researcher comes to understand the world.

A theme of *College Academics* is that when discussing socialisation it is often difficult to determine what is the cause of current behaviour – current circumstances or something that occurred elsewhere. Thus when examining the reasons for starting the research that ultimately led to this book, it is hard to know how far to go back in history. In a sense too my own biography is bound up with those in this book. Many of the issues that apply to these academics apply to me, too, as readers of *College Academics* would readily observe.

Biographical influences

Attending a small rural high school, I was one of two pupils in my year who went on to university. I won a Teachers' College Scholarship to the University of New England in Armidale. The scholarship was initially for four years. However, in my fourth year I was contacted by the Principal of Armidale Teachers' College, Paul Lamb, to say that he was recommending that two others and I be given an extension of scholarship to complete a Master of Education. Unfortunately, changes at the end of the year meant that Paul Lamb ceased to have any responsibility for those he had recommended for extension of scholarship. The new administrative unit that was given responsibility for us knew nothing of Lamb's recommendation. There followed an anxious week until finally his original decision was confirmed. This was my first real taste of the twin characteristics of teaching in the New South Wales Department of Education – a typical bureaucracy of the time. On the one hand there were caring and wonderful human beings like Lamb, and on the other the faceless bureaucracy that was the New South Wales Department of Education. This critical incident would later help me to empathise with the individuals in *College Academics* who spoke of the disillusionment that working with Australian education bureaucracies had caused them.

My time at the University of New England was happy and stimulating. What struck me was that the academic staff there enjoyed considerable personal and occupational freedom. I decided that I would like an academic career. However, a wonderful Scotsman, James Dolan, who lectured me in medieval history, gave me some friendly advice in 1972. He cautioned me that the academic game was finished' and that I should not contemplate such a career.

The great majority of my first degree was in history. Many of the units I studied concentrated on the study of particular individuals. Thus, my interest was focussed on individuals in history. At the end of my Masters degree I went into secondary school teaching, and was fortunate to be offered a position in the town of Taree on the sought-after New South Wales north coast. However, after a few weeks I was transferred a short distance to Wingham. Most teachers would have killed for such first postings. Despite the attractions, having been transferred so soon in my career made me realise that there would be very few career freedoms working in the New South Wales Department of Education. Consequently, when offered a position at Bendigo State College I accepted it. My school teaching experience later enabled me to understand the life histories of those I interviewed for *College Academics*.

The position at Bendigo, I reasoned, would maximise my personal and professional satisfaction. Indeed, on my arrival I soon observed that many of the staff had seemingly unlimited freedom in carrying out their role. Soon after arrival at Bendigo I undertook a Diploma in Tertiary Education. Interestingly, there was not much encouragement from the College to do this; my feeling was that it did not excessively value teaching ability despite its official position. This theme later emerged in *College Academics*. An unexpected outcome of my completing the diploma was that I became interested in qualitative methodology and symbolic interactionism. For one course requirement I undertook a small-scale study of two new Bendigo staff members, and this started my interest in the study of academic careers.

American academics: then and now

The particular impetus that made me especially interested in researching academics was my reading of Logan Wilson's *American Academics: Then and Now*. Wilson (1979) noted that *American Academics* was a belated follow-up of his first study into the American academic profession. He observed that sociologists of the era when he wrote his first book had written on an array of occupational types. However, he was unable to locate any prototype for studying a higher level profession. Subsequently he believed that prospective academics and members of the profession might be interested in the findings.

Wilson went on to quote three amusing pieces that were especially influential in making me want to study academics. The first was from the *Wall Street Journal* of 11 August 1970, by an Edwin Harwood, and was entitled *Confessions of a Conservative Sociologist'* (Wilson, 1979, p. 13). Harwood claimed that:

Students see that their professors can take time off any time of the day to run errands, and that instead of the one-and-a-half or two-day weekend, they can arrange a teaching schedule that will give them three or even four days ... classes can be cancelled or rescheduled. Naturally many students would like to have the same freedom for themselves.

Later Wilson (1979, p. 199) referred to a book published by an anonymous Professor X entitled *This Beats Working for a Living: The Dark Secrets of a College Professor*. Wilson noted a quotation from another unnamed professor: The life of a well-established, middle-aged professor in the Arts Faculty of a modern university can, if he likes to make it so, be one of the softest jobs to be found on the earth's surface'.

Wilson also recorded some remarks by J. Kenneth Galbraith. In 1976 Galbraith was given $US10,000 in cash and a purple and gold Cadillac by the campus *Humour Magazine* for being Harvard's funniest professor in 100 years. Wilson records Galbraith's humorous acceptance speech at the ceremony. It included these remarks:

An aspect of grim harassment also suggests deep devotion to one's work; gaiety, in contrast, could be thought to imply idleness. This is important because Harvard may be the only considerable community in the world, the Pentagon possibly excepted, where the effort to stimulate effort can exceed effort itself. After three months' vacation in the summer, a professor takes a sabbatical leave in the autumn so that he will be rested and ready for a winter's leave of absence to work up a course on the work ethic.

This reading of Wilson's *American Academics* gave me further impetus and enthusiasm to study college academics. I also gained some more specific research questions to do with occupational choice as they applied to academics.

Why study my own institution?

For a number of reasons academic staff at Bendigo College of Advanced Education were chosen for the research that finally appeared as *College Academics*. They were close by, and this was a not unimportant consideration. Interest in the research topic was also stimulated by what appeared to be differences in the way various staff perceived their role and the differences in the nature of their commitment. Most important was the comment by my first Head of School that Bendigo College always experienced difficulty in recruiting staff.

Bendigo College had been formed from the merger of a teacher training institution and an institute of technology. The merger, coupled with contractions in the whole of higher education in Australia during the late 1970s and 1980s, had had an unsettling effect on staff. For example, during the late 1970s and early 1980s a number of staff expressed the desire to move to a university where they believed conditions would be better. Some of those who resigned had the highest academic qualifications, and resigned with no position to go to.

Production issues

Personal and professional

A critical point in turning the research that I had done on Bendigo academic staff into *College Academics* occurred when I received notice of the *17th International Standing Conference for the History of Education,* to be held in Berlin, Germany, in September 1995. The theme was Education Studies, and there was a section concerned with the profession of education. This was an area that I had data on from my interviews with staff at Bendigo. I wrote a proposal that was accepted. I then presented another paper from my research to the *18th International Standing Conference for the History of Education* in Cracow, Poland, in August 1996. Sometime later this was published in the British journal *Educational Studies,* and was also selected for publication in another edited work. It was while on my way to the conference in Cracow that I met the publisher of my book.

Following this I gave papers that were ultimately to form parts of *College Academics* in Amsterdam at a conference on *Universities and their Cities,* and in California at a conference entitled *Reclaiming Voice.* These conference presentations encouraged me to proceed with turning my research data into a book. The support that I received at these international meetings from supportive peers was crucial in my decision. Writing *College Academics* was also to some extent my attempt to reclaim control over my life and to create a new one. There was also a wish to do it for my children, and hence the dedication in the front of the book – To the 3 Js (my children Jason, Jodie and Justin).

Institutional

There were other influences that contributed to the final publication of *College Academics*. At the time of the conference in Berlin I was informed that my Head of School wanted me to resume being Head of Education Studies and to take over coordination of the Masters of Education degree. My best efforts to thwart his plans failed. Somewhat later, while congratulating me on exceeding our student numbers, he added that he wanted me to increase my involvement in research. Initially I did nothing to comply with his request. However, I noticed that there were attractions that came with research and publication. These included conference attendance, travel, a reduced teaching load, and having colleagues in various parts of Australia and the world. Finally my Head of School, when reviewing workloads, found my teaching load was excessive. Consequently he offered me a reduced load or help with assessing student work. This was a very important factor in the writing of *College Academics*.

Historiographical

I wanted *College Academics* to be a study of people and not simply of an institution. I was influenced first by the claims of one of my former teachers (Bowen, 1973, pp. 10–22), who noted deficiencies in the study of the history of Australian education. In a provocative piece he claimed that there was too great a concentration on support systems with little attention to pedagogy and ideology.

Second I was influenced by Theobald (1977, p. 22), who wrote of the problems of writing school histories. I reasoned that many of her comments about school histories applied to at least some of the institutional histories of higher education. Theobald noted that school histories have long been a blight upon the landscape of historical scholarship ... most have little interest beyond their nostalgic appeal to ex-pupils'.

Theobald noted that the issue in writing good histories of

educational institutions was in formulating alternative methods of attack'. Such histories had to break out of the hot house atmosphere of adulation and self-congratulation' and find a way to examine the mystique of the institution (Theobald, 1977, p. 22). There was a need to question whether certain aims and values that were espoused at the official level were realised, to move beyond unquestioning acceptance of the aims and values of the institution and to delve wider than the administrative level of the institution's existence, Theobald also noted that anyone reading the history should have an inkling of what it felt like to be there'.

The problems of examining my own institution were further highlighted by an advertisement that appeared in *The Age* newspaper, published in Melbourne. This advertisement was placed by the private school, Wesley College, when seeking a historian to write its history. The advertisement noted (Wesley College, 1996):

> The Historian will be required to write a first class history of Wesley College as a *ground breaking and influential educational institution.* [and] will ... *contribute to the marketing and public relations activities associated with the subject* (my emphasis).

I certainly did not want my work to be constrained in this manner. I knew, as C. Wallace (1997, p. 13), unauthorised biographer of Germaine Greer, had noted, that

> ... there is a huge risk that authorised will mean compromised [and] this jeopardises the fundamental obligation to ethical behaviour and truthfulness incumbent on all writers dealing with the real world. These are obligations to readers as well as to subjects and sources.

My own research was particularly influenced by a number of studies on Australian Colleges of Advanced Education. These studies appeared from 1975 until 1986 (Anderson *et al.*, 1975; Harman *et al.*, 1985; Harman, 1986). The researchers noted that they had selected colleges for study, as there was a lack of research on them compared to universities (Anderson *et al.*, 1975). However, they then set about making some comparisons with overseas academics as they claimed comparisons with

Australian university academics are difficult because few serious studies have been made to date' (Anderson *et al.*, 1975, p. 3). I noted that this disparity was seized upon by some Bendigo College staff and added to their feelings of unease when the research was published. Staff asked why colleges, as opposed to universities, had been selected for study. They believed that the researchers had found it much easier to gain access to Colleges of Advanced Education through their college councils, and a more friendly and accessible staff, than it would have been to gain access to universities. For these staff this was an example of the studying down' that Coffey (1996, pp. 61–63) refers to. I noted that the researchers (Anderson *et al.*, 1975) themselves were not completely unaware of this.

Meek's (1984) classic case study of an Australian College of Advanced Education was particularly influential in my work. This was an excellent study of institutional professional life. A key theme was the change of an institution from a state-run bureaucratic organisation to an independent self-governing one. At the time of his research on Gippsland Institute of Advanced Education, Meek was a member of the University of Melbourne's Centre for the Study of Higher Education. Also working there was a higher education specialist, Grant Harman, who wrote the preface to Meek's work. I was troubled (rightly or wrongly) that there was too much of the great men of history' in Meek's work, and that it had some of the problems to which Theobald (1977) had alluded. For example, in the preface Harman (Meek, 1984, p. ix) notes that to a substantial extent the tyranny of distance has been substantially overcome by the introduction of external studies programs, which were the brainchild of the foundation director, Max Hooper'. Harman continues:

> The quality, high community standing, and prestige of regional colleges have been largely the result of the foresight, dedication, and hard work of a small group of highly committed leaders. Many of the colleges were indeed fortunate in their choice of foundation directors.

There was no mention of ordinary staff members here. What about all their efforts in building Australia's College of Advanced Education system?

I was also alerted to the fact that higher education institutions may proclaim a disinterested search for the truth, but, like any commercial organisation that protects its secrets, they have ways and means of silencing their critics. More recently, the work of Armstrong, a British researcher, warned me that universities are selective in what they want to hear from studies on themselves (personal communication, 1997). The parts that are good public relations for universities are well received by university managers. However, the problem, according to Armstrong, is that some parts (for example those that deal with problematic issues) are negative in their impact and it is these that tend to get suppressed by the university managers.

Theoretical

In writing *College Academics* I wondered it if was just going to be how Berger (1963, p. 19) had described much of the sociological enterprise – namely another little study of obscure fragments of social life, irrelevant to any broader theoretical concerns. Following on from this I was influenced by Spaull, who writes of the biographical tradition in the history of Australian education. He (Spaull, 1981, pp. 3–5) suggested the use of concepts from sociology to write contemporary and participant history. He also suggested one should 'write biographies of the ordinary or anonymous people in schooling as well as collective biographies of these groups'. His observation that the biographical tradition in the history of education would enable me to approach my study in a humanistic way suggested that I should utilise concepts and methods from areas such as socialisation theory where these were applicable. However, I was also aware of Simon's aversion to the use of sociological theory. She noted (Simon, 1983, p. 9) that such theorising has people pushed and pulled around by external pressures, lacking a complex capacity to learn, and without self-activity.

In spite of my alertness to Simon's (1973) concerns, symbolic interactionism offered a framework for *College Academics* that focussed on the individual in career choice and in institutional life. I noted Woods' observation that symbolic interactionism contrasts markedly with theories that claim that human behaviour is determined by structural forces in society. Interactionism was a pertinent framework for me to use as it emphasises these college academics as constructors, creators and copers who continually interacted with the world and were influenced by and influenced the world (Woods, 1992, p. 338).

I was also influenced by Hage and Powers (1992, p. 208) who suggested combining useful insights from different theoretical schools to produce a viable analytical scheme for studying the meso level of social organisation, where individuals are influenced by and in turn influence the character of a social order that extends beyond themselves'. They also suggested to me the need for an eclectic form of symbolic interactionism, which notes the need for more flexible social institutions, complex selves, and creative minds'. They stressed that, because of technological change, social roles and selves are becoming more complex and the definition of behaviour, of duties and of obligations in roles are becoming more open, more subject to the effects of human agency, than ever before'.

Burgess (1995) noted the central place of ethnographic studies of educational institutions and how studies by major researchers are indebted to the pioneering work of Becker. He (1995, p. 15) noted that Becker's work is as relevant for sociology and sociologists in the 1990s as when it was first published'. Burgess stressed Becker's seminal contributions to studies of socialisation, particularly his development of the concepts of situational adjustment, perspectives and commitment – concepts I utilised.

Theobald encapsulates the problems that I faced. The challenge was to tell the story of these academics, but to invest their stories with the wider significance which transforms them into theoretical knowledge' (Theobald, 1998, p. 31). She noted that she tried to make this work at two levels in her *Knowing Women*: both for the general reader and for the specialist reader who would review the book (Theobald, 1998, p. 31). She noted how she consciously set out to balance theory and narrative/biography, sometimes between chapters and sometimes within chapters'. Interestingly, she observes the average reader would find two chapters difficult to understand'.

Thus *College Academics* used a theoretical framework partly due to the academic subculture of which I found myself a part. Of course I could have done a conventional history, and there are exemplars of these. Ultimately, too, symbolic interactionism was a hard theory to master; not only for me but also for some of the reviewers, as is noted later on.

Research

While undertaking the research for the book I was never denied material by anyone in authority at Bendigo College and had no trouble getting access to written sources. Being an insider also meant that I found material that I presume others may never have found. For example, I discovered material in the archives to do with staffing issues that I am sure outside researchers would have been denied access to. I should probably not have been allowed to read the material myself. Having said that, much of it I did not directly use as it was confidential. However, the material provided a useful perspective on how I interpreted other data.

My unrestricted access was probably due to my research identity as a lone wolf researcher' (Punch, 1994, p. 87). I was already a member of the institution I was studying, did not require any funding, and melted away into the field – in contrast to the hired hand', who would be highly visible, tied to contractual obligations and expected to deliver a report in a certain time frame (Punch, 1994, p. 87). I also knew that issues concerned with reporting my findings could cause me problems.

Self-censorship also occurred. This involved the following incident, which revolved around the rapidly changing context that Bendigo College and the whole of Australian higher education found itself facing in the 1980s. In 1981 the Director of Bendigo College conducted a campaign to preserve engineering courses at Bendigo despite government attempts to close them. Finally, the Director succeeded in having some of the courses preserved. It was suggested that the College's resident cartoonist draw up a cartoon of the Director getting off a plane waving his umbrella with in the other hand a piece of paper, and proclaiming Engineering in Our Time'. The cartoonist somewhat reluctantly drew the said cartoon and submitted it to the College Newsletter, which the Director edited. The cartoon never appeared and was never seen again. Initially I was going to use this as an example of how the institutional view was carefully controlled by key personnel in the College. I discussed this with a number of Bendigo staff, and got various reactions that ranged from mild amusement to disdain. Ultimately I left the instance out. In hindsight, I should have included it.

Other incidents that occurred during the research for the book stand out. There is one in particular that serves as a warning to inside researchers that their past activities can return to haunt them. I was interviewing a very helpful staff member and had asked him whether there were any particular disappointments in his career. He answered that there were two major ones; the first was the lack of promotion opportunities, and the second was that a motion of no confidence had been moved in him when he was President of the Academic Staff Association. He added: 'And you would remember that well'. I did when he mentioned it, as I had been the person who seconded the motion. I have never felt so embarrassed in my life.

Along with needing a fairly thick skin for self-inflicted incidents such as the above, I found that a small minority of staff I interviewed were particularly rude and offensive. These staff made very disparaging remarks about my colleagues in the area that I worked in, and about the whole of educational research generally. The only thing to do in these situations was to 'grin and bear it'. Once they had unburdened themselves of these ideas they were willing to be interviewed at length and were friendly and helpful. Above all, what really stands out was how incredibly open the staff were in what they told me during their interviews.

Writing

The writing of *College Academics* was hard work. Compounding this were my own feelings of isolation. I had almost no one locally to talk to about my work. However, perhaps this forced me just to get on and write. Endless discussions with others might have advanced the writing process or they might have become just another form of avoidance behaviour substituting for the hard task of writing.

I ended up with a huge mass of transcript, archival and other field-note data. After sorting this into some sort of manageable structure I had to find a way of ordering it, and after coding it I attempted to link the various questions and pieces of data into some sort of story line. Then I developed a coherent and readable narrative. This I vividly remember as it took me many months of being locked in solitary confinement trying to piece all the data into some overall structure. Having done this I thought the hard part was finished; I now at least had an account that hung together. How wrong I was.

The next phase was much more difficult. I had to see how my descriptive account of these academics' lives could be explained in terms of my symbolic interactionist framework. Anyone who alleges that *College Academics* is positivistic does not know the sheer agony of the process that involved seeing if symbolic interactionism could in fact explain the narrative that I had constructed. It took many months before my narrative and my theoretical framework appeared to coalesce into a unified whole. Finally the overall outline of the book emerged, with chapters that focussed on occupational choice, institutional and occupational socialisation, perspectives on teaching, research, and commitment.

Self doubts

While writing *College Academics* I had recurrent doubts as to whether there was any value in doing it. Such misgivings were not only about this book having any value, but also concerned the worth of the whole of the social sciences. It kept occurring to me that I was living a somewhat rarefied existence and that academic work was somehow not real work. I did not have to labour like many people around me. True enough, though, there was heartache and pain in writing.

I did not fully understand these fears until I attended the *Second Working Class Academics' Conference* at Newburgh, New York, in 1996. On this occasion I heard a speaker talk of the difficulty she had in convincing her grandparents that she did real work at a university. Real work was indeed reading, research and writing; real work did not have to be the hard manual labour of the working classes.

Perseverance

During the research for (and especially the writing of) *College Academics* I became particularly aware of Berger's (1963, p. 12) pithy observation that normal academic life is a jungle of bitter warfare between faculty factions, none of which can be relied upon for an objective judgement of members of either his [*sic*] or an opposing group'. Being basically a nervous and insecure person, I needed something to keep me going. A number of things helped me to persevere with writing *College Academics*. Most important of these was the reading of Punch's study on the politics of research. Within his account, two instances in particular gave me determination to continue. His 1994 account of Whyte's trouble in publishing what turned out to be his *Street Corner Society* (1943), having it reviewed and seriously accepted, and how its fluctuating sales have reflected the rise and fall of various fads and fashions of sociology, was especially motivating. I also drew some reassurance from the fact that acceptance of his research for a doctorate at Chicago was due to Hughes promoting him against a critical Wirth (Punch, 1994, p. 87).

I also drew determination to keep going from the history of Humphrey's work. He (Punch, 1994, pp. 88–89) had used questionable research tactics to study homosexual encounters, but had received the coveted C. Wright Mills Award, forbore efforts to have his PhD revoked and had an irate Alvin Gouldner physically attack him. Thus I came to see that even the great and the good in academic life were just mortals like the rest of us. My reaction was: Well if the academic world can find room for this kind of behaviour and reward parts of it then perhaps there is a small place for me too'.

Response

Local and institutional

When I had a draft of the book completed the institution I worked in (and the one that the book is about) announced it would be holding a 125 Years Anniversary Celebration of Tertiary Education in Bendigo. Consequently, expressions of interest were invited for the writing of a corporate history of the former Bendigo College. I was not interested in writing such a work. However, I sent two chapters of *College Academics* to the organising committee to see if they were interested. They were not and could not find anyone on the staff who was able to write their book. An outside writer was commissioned to produce the work, which ended up being 27 pages in length with very attractive photos (R. Wallace, 1997). When my work was finally released, the author of the corporate history purchased a copy and came to ask if I would autograph it for him. We had a long conversation about the issues that he had faced in writing his work. He confirmed that he had been heavily censored and had had to leave out contentious issues.

Hence, my suspicions initially evoked by Meek's (1984) work were reconfirmed. Had I stepped out of line in what I wrote in *College Academics*, I would have found life difficult. Lest it be thought that these kinds of pressures only apply at ordinary institutions', notice should be taken of Roberts' (1998, p. 101) account of his taking up the Vice-Chancellorship at Southampton University in the United Kingdom. He recounts that on arrival he went to the official history of the university for information but noted it became more bland and uninformative the closer it got to the present time. More interestingly, he found in an interleaved version in a locked drawer in the vice-chancellor's office passages interpolated by the author on more recent events that he considered too risky to commit to the printed page.

On the other hand, the organising committee in Bendigo graciously included brochures of my book in their publicity distributed for the anniversary celebrations. *The Bendigo Advertiser* newspaper did a feature review, and the local radio station ran a news item on it. Overall at my institution the reaction was muted when the book was released. Around ten persons complimented me on writing it. The Foundation Director of the Bendigo College of Advanced Education congratulated me on producing it. When Tight's (1999) review appeared, my Head of School sent me a congratulatory e-mail and my Head of Department personally congratulated me. How he found out about the review escapes me. The bookshop manager said that large numbers of staff came in simply to read the book without purchasing it.

The release of *College Academics* did cause some tense moments where I worked. During a workshop session one of the staff I had interviewed for the book came up to me and said: I expect you are making large amounts from your book. How about giving royalties to those that you interviewed'? He continued: You would never get ethics permission to do such a study now'. He was quite agitated and I tried to pacify him. I later discovered that he had allegedly identified himself in the book and did not like what he saw. Why, I do not know – the supposed portrayal was in fact complimentary. I was extremely nervous that if he made a fuss it could make my life at the institution somewhat unpleasant.

A former staff member and a present one commented that

they thought *College Academics* was far too positive. I thought long and hard over these comments, as they raised the issue that Theobald (1977) noted in asking, how well does the book capture the institution? I had not written a typical institutional history, but the tone that the book created was important. One of the people who had made a comment was now in a senior position in another university. On re-reading my field notes and transcripts it became clear that he had enjoyed a very light teaching load and very favourable terms and conditions while employed at Bendigo. However, an extremely ambitious character perhaps helps to explain his belief that I was too positive in my portrayal. I would argue that *College Academics* is not a particularly positive account. Much of the story is one of lost opportunities, lack of foresight, lack of motivation and application by some staff. Not all saw the story that the book told as positive, with Stortz (1998) in particular seeing it as a rather depressing tale.

Professional and international

Reviews of *College Academics* appeared in Canada, (where it was book of the month in the *Canadian Association of University Teachers' Bulletin* (Stortz, 1998)), in Australia (Davis, 1998), and in the United Kingdom (Burns, 1999; Tight, 1999). The reviews were generous and positive and highlighted the contributions to knowledge that *College Academics* makes. At the worst, one reviewer got my name incorrect, some factual details wrong and positively loathed the effect of the theoretical framework on the story that was told. Davis, a mainstream historian of education, found the theoretical framework of *College Academics* was not to his liking, claiming that facts are presented in what might appear to some readers as overly-complex jargon, which does little to advance the argument'.

Stortz too noted that ùndoubtedly the most inaccessible part of the book to the sociologically uninitiated is the vernacular of symbolic interactionism'. However, he is more forgiving and tolerant, noting that a careful reading of the first three introductory/methodology chapters makes this hurdle of specialised jargon much less onerous [and] ultimately, issues applicable to academic identity and how academics adapted to their occupational world [are] elucidated for any interdisciplinary audience'.

Having found solace in the comments of Stortz, I am still, as I presume others are, troubled by the language of much of the area that I work in. In particular, I have in mind a recent report by Kelly (1999, p. 2) headed Deep and Meaningless', where he notes that it may be nonsense, but in the language of academe you'd never know'.

Personal

One of the most significant discoveries in *College Academics* was that many academic staff at Bendigo became academics for non-academic reasons; rather for associated life-style reasons. This could ultimately cause these individuals, their occupations and their institutions difficulties in terms of lack of commitment, dissatisfaction and low morale. From a methodological perspective I learnt to approach my next study differently. Specifically, I had a much sharper focus at the start and was much clearer about possible directions that the study could take.

Having now commenced a study looking at local perspectives on regional universities, I am even more acutely aware of how changing research climates influence the research process. Gaining permission to undertake *College Academics* was much easier then than it is to do similar sorts of research today. Now it is much harder to locate seemingly non-threatening information at my institution. Changed times and changed circumstances mean that my university (and I presume many others) makes it even harder to gain access to information.

Conclusion

The above critical commentary on the research for and writing of *College Academics* belongs to the reflective research genre. Such an analysis was not easily done by me, and indeed other researchers and writers note a reluctance to undertake such work (Theobald, 1998, p. 29). This critical commentary entailed disclosures that academics are not always willing to make by isolating key aspects in the research for and the writing of *College Academics*. The most important of these are summarised below.

My personal realities were important for the choice of the research topic and the direction of the research that formed *College Academics*. The origins of the book are intimately connected with my biography and extend to my university experience as a student and personal observations that I made then of academic life. It was partly through myself that I came to understand the world of these academics. Of particular importance in influencing my study was my reading of Wilson's (1979) *American Academics: Then and Now*. This work provided me with the enthusiasm to start the study with a theoretical and methodological approach.

College Academics was influenced by a desire to move away from the more conventional institutional history to a more analytical history of individual academics. The approach taken was heavily influenced by some classic studies of college academics and higher education institutions in Australia. I was wary of aspects of these, and wanted to avoid the 'great persons of history approach'. Because I was studying professional occupations I drew on the classic studies of occupational socialisation of the Chicago School of Symbolic Interactionism. While it has its roots in the America of the 1930s, the framework has undergone continuous development and refinement and is still pertinent today. What I aimed to do was to invest the stories of these college academics with wider significance, which turned them into theoretical knowledge (Theobald, 1998, p. 31).

Especially important in turning the research into the final book were conference presentations that I made at *The International Standing Conference for the History of Education* in various overseas cities. Of particular importance was the support and encouragement of key writers and researchers that I met at these conferences. In conjunction with these international professional influences were local institutional factors at my own university, including directives and support from my Head of School. I also drew encouragement from reading 'tales of the field' (Punch, 1994) and the accounts of important classic studies that had been conducted of institutions and occupations.

The response to *College Academics* occurred at a number of levels. At my own institution its release coincided with anniversary celebrations of tertiary education in Bendigo and the release of a more traditional corporate history (Wallace, 1997). The research approaches for the two books, while completely different, also encountered similar problems of what could and could not be included and how to deal with local institutional sensitivities. When *College Academics* was released, the local reaction ranged from compliments to concern by one academic at his alleged portrayal. The latter incident illustrated how researchers are never completely free from their research, as issues can occur and continue once the finished work is released to the wider public.

Very importantly, the process of researching and writing *College Academics* meant that I was socialised into the academic world that I was writing about. Writing *College Academics* meant that my academic self altered to broaden my role from purely teaching to one involving research, conference presentations and writing. Writing *College Academics* was akin to becoming a member of a tribe and gaining tribe membership (Becher, 1989).

References

Aitken, D. (1999) Degrees of crisis. *The Australian,* April 7: 34.

Anderson, D. S., Batt, K. J., Beswick, D. G. and Harman, G. S. (1975) *Regional Colleges – A Study of Non-Metropolitan Colleges of Advanced Education in Australia, Vols 1–3.* Canberra: Australian National University Press.

Becher, T. (1989) *Academic Tribes and Territories.* Milton Keynes: SRHE and Open University Press.

Berger, P. (1963) *Invitation to Sociology.* Harmondsworth: Pelican.

Blumer, H. (1969) *Symbolic Interactionism – Perspective and Method.* Englewood Cliffs, NJ: Prentice Hall Inc.

Bowen, J. (1973) The persistence of the liberal arts in the concept of the educated man. *Australian and New Zealand History of Education Journal* 2(2): 10–22.

Burns, R. (1999) Review of Anthony Potts, *College Academics* Charlestown NSW: William Michael Press. *Comparative Education* 35(3): 355–356.

Burgess, R. (ed.) (1995) *Howard Becker on Education.* Bristol: Open University Press.

Coffey, A. (1996) The power of accounts: authority and authorship in ethnography. *Qualitative Studies in Education* 9(1): 61–74.

Davis, R. (1998) Review of: *College Academics. History of Education Review* 27(2): 70–71.

Delamont, S. (1998) Review of: *On Writing Qualitative Research: Living By Words. British Educational Research Journal* 24: 365.

Fitz, J. and Halpin, D. (1994) Ministers and mandarins: Educational research in elite settings. *In:* G. Walford (ed.), *Researching the Powerful in Education,* pp. 32–50. London: University College London Press.

Hage, J. and Powers, C. H. (1992) *Post-Industrial Lives – Roles and Relationships in the 21st Century.* London: Sage.

Harman, G. D., Beswick, H. and Schofield, J. (1985) *The Amalgamation of Colleges of Advanced Education at Ballarat and Bendigo*. Melbourne: The University of Melbourne Centre for the Study of Higher Education.

Harman, G. S. (1986) Mergers in higher education: combining and integrating two colleges of advanced education at Bendigo. *In*: I. Palmer (ed.), *Melbourne Studies in Education*, pp. 180–208. Carlton: Melbourne University Press.

Kelly, R. (1999) Deep and meaningless. *The Age – Saturday Extra*, May: 2.

Marginson, S. (1998) Review of: *The Mockers and the Mocked: Comparative Perspectives on Differentiation, Convergence and Diversity in Higher Education*. *Studies in Higher Education* 23(1): 103–104.

McCalman, J. (1996) *Towns and Gowns: The Humanities and the Community*. Bendigo: La Trobe University.

McNamara, D. R. (1980) The outsider's arrogance: the failure of participant observers to understand classroom events. *British Educational Research Journal* 6(2): 113–125.

Meek, V. L. (1984) *Brown Coal or Plato? – A Study of the Gippsland of Advanced Education*. Melbourne: ACER.

Meek, V. L., Goedegebuure, L., Kivinen, O. and Rinne, R. (eds) (1996) *The Mockers and Mocked: Comparative Perspectives on Differentiation, Convergence and Diversity in Higher Education*. Oxford: Pergamon Press.

Potts, A. (1997) *College Academics*. Charlestown, NH: William Michael Press.

Punch, M. (1994) Politics and ethics in qualitative research. *In*: N. K. Denzin and Y. S. Lincoln (eds), *Handbook of Qualitative Research*, pp. 83–97. London: Sage.

Roberts, J. M. (1998) Recollections of a pre-revolution. *Oxford Review of Education* 24(1): 99–110.

Simon, J. (1983) The history of education and the hew' social history. *History of Education Review* 12(2): 1–15.

Spaull, A. (1981) The biographical tradition in the history of Australian education. *Australia and New Zealand History of Education Society Journal* 10(2): 1–10.

Stortz, P. (1998) New perspectives on the professoriate down under. *CAUT ACPPN Bulletin* 45(8): 7.

Theobald, M. (1977) Problems in writing school histories. *Australian and New Zealand History of Education Society Journal* 6(1): 22–28.

Theobald, M. (1998) Writing landscapes for a good teacher. *History of Education Review* 27(2): 29–36.

Tight, M. (1999) Review of: *College Academics. Studies in Higher Education* 24(1): 127–128.

Wallace, C. (1997) Unauthorised, uncompromised. *The Australian* 22 October: 13.

Wallace, R. (1997) *Inkpots to Internet – Celebrating 125 Years of Tertiary Education in Bendigo*. Bendigo, La Trobe University, Bendigo and Bendigo Regional Institute of Tafe.

Wesley College (1996) Advertisement for School Historian. *The Age Extra*, December 14: 8.

Wilson, L. (1979) *American Academics: Then and Now*. New York, NY: Oxford University Press.

Woods, P. (1992) Symbolic interactionism: theory and method. *In*: W. Millroy and J. Preissle (eds), *The Handbook of Qualitative Research in Education*, pp. 337–404. San Diego, CA: Academic Press.

Woods, P. (1996) *Research in the Art of Teaching: Ethnography for Educational Use*. London: Routledge.

Index